Rabbits

Our Best Friends

The Boxer

Caring for Your Mutt

The German Shepherd

The Golden Retriever

The Labrador Retriever

The Poodle

The Shih Tzu

The Yorkshire Terrier

Ferrets

Gerbils

Guinea Pigs

Hamsters

Lizards

Rabbits

Snakes

Turtles

OUR BEST FRIENDS

Rabbits

Janice Biniok

ELDORADO INK

Produced by OTTN Publishing, Stockton, New Jersey

Eldorado Ink
PO Box 100097
Pittsburgh, PA 15233
www.eldoradoink.com

First printing

1 3 5 7 9 8 6 4 2

Library of Congress Cataloging-in-Publication Data

Biniok, Janice.
  Rabbits / Janice Biniok.
      p. cm. — (Our best friends)
    ISBN 978-1-932904-32-1 (hardcover) — ISBN 978-1-932904-40-6 (trade ed.)
  1. Rabbits—Juvenile literature. I. Title.
  SF453.2.B55 2008
  636.932'2—dc22

                                        2008038521

Photo credits: Courtesy The American Rabbit Breeders Association, Inc., 37;
Courtesy Richard Graham, 50, 51, 100; ©iStockphoto.com/Ana Abejon, 72;
©iStockphoto.com/Rosemarie Gearhart, 21; ©iStockphoto.com/Klaus Nilkens, 101;
©iStockphoto.com/Vicki Stephenson, 64; ©iStockphoto.com/Nicola Stratford, 42; Courtesy
PetSitters.org, 97; Used under license from Shutterstock, Inc., 3, 8, 12, 15, 16, 17, 19, 22, 24,
25, 27, 30, 33, 34, 35, 38, 39, 44, 46, 48, 53, 55, 56, 58, 62, 66, 67, 68, 70, 74, 75, 79, 82, 84,
87, 88, 90, 93, 96, "Fun Fact" icon image, Cover (all images, front and back).

TABLE OF CONTENTS

Introduction

The mutually beneficial relationship between humans and animals began long before the dawn of recorded history. Archaeologists believe that humans began to capture and tame wild goats, sheep, and pigs more than 9,000 years ago. These animals were then bred for specific purposes, such as providing humans with a reliable source of food or providing furs and hides that could be used for clothing or the construction of dwellings.

Other animals had been sought for companionship and assistance even earlier. The dog, believed to be the first animal domesticated, began living and working with Stone Age humans in Europe more than 14,000 years ago. Some archaeologists believe that wild dogs and humans were drawn together because both hunted the same prey. By taming and training dogs, humans became more effective hunters. Dogs, meanwhile, enjoyed the social contact with humans and benefited from greater access to food and warm shelter. Dogs soon became beloved pets as well as trusted workers. This can be seen from the many artifacts depicting dogs that have been found at ancient sites in Asia, Europe, North America, and the Middle East.

The earliest domestic cats appeared in the Middle East about 5,000 years ago. Small wild cats were probably first attracted to human settlements because plenty of rodents could be found wherever harvested grain was stored. Cats played a useful role in hunting and killing these pests, and it is likely that grateful humans rewarded them for this assistance. Over time, these small cats gave up some of their aggressive wild behaviors and began living among humans. Cats eventually became so popular in ancient Egypt that they were believed to possess magical powers. Cat statues were placed outside homes to ward off evil spirits, and mummified cats were included in royal tombs to accompany their owners into the afterlife.

Today, few people believe that cats have supernatural powers, but most pet owners feel a magical bond with their pets, whether they are dogs, cats, hamsters, rabbits, horses, or parrots. The lives of pets and their people become inextricably intertwined, providing strong emotional and physical rewards for both humans and animals. People of all ages can benefit from the loving companionship of a pet. Not surprisingly, then, pet ownership is widespread. Recent statistics indicate that about 60 percent of all households in the United States and Canada have at least one pet, while the figure is close to 50 percent of households in the United Kingdom. For millions of people, therefore, pets truly have become their "best friends."

Finding the best animal friend can be a challenge, however. Not only are there many types of domesticated pets, but each has specific needs, characteristics, and personality traits. Even within a category of pets, such as dogs, different breeds will flourish in different surroundings and with different treatment. For example, a German Shepherd may not be the right pet for a person living in a cramped urban apartment; that person might be better off caring for a smaller dog like a Toy Poodle or Shih Tzu, or perhaps a cat. On the other hand, an active person who loves the outdoors may prefer the companion-ship of a Labrador Retriever to that of a small dog or a passive indoor pet like a goldfish or hamster.

The joys of pet ownership come with certain responsibilities. Bringing a pet into your home and your neighborhood obligates you to care for and train the pet properly. For example, a dog must be housebroken, taught to obey your commands, and trained to behave appropriately when he encounters other people or animals. Owners must also be mindful of their pet's particular nutritional and medical needs.

The purpose of the OUR BEST FRIENDS series is to provide a helpful and comprehensive introduction to pet ownership. Each book contains the basic information a prospective pet owner needs in order to choose the right pet for his or her situation and to care for that pet throughout the pet's lifetime. Training, socialization, proper nutrition, potential medical issues, and the legal responsibilities of pet ownership are thoroughly explained and discussed, and an abundance of expert tips and suggestions are offered. Whether it is a hamster, corn snake, guinea pig, or Labrador Retriever, the books in the OUR BEST FRIENDS series provide everything the reader needs to know about how to have a happy, well-adjusted, and well-behaved pet.

Rabbits can make wonderful pets because they are social animals. A wide variety of rabbit breeds, each with differences in size and coat quality, are available.

CHAPTER ONE

Is a Rabbit Right for You?

Rabbits have been portrayed in many different lights. Easter bunnies are known to be industrious little fellows. Peter Rabbit is synonymous with adventure and mischief. Bugs Bunny is as clever as a fox, but much funnier. So what is a real rabbit like? The truth is, rabbits are a little bit of each. They are industrious, adventuresome, mischievous, clever, and funny!

It's hard to believe so much personality can fit into such a small body, but that's what makes rabbits so endearing. Add to this the fact that they are cute, cuddly, and wrapped in a covering of fur that is softer than anything else on earth, and you can understand why rabbits are such popular pets. How can anyone resist the temptation to own one, hold one, and pet one?

Deciding if a rabbit is the right pet for you isn't a matter of determining whether rabbits have what it takes as animal companions. Rabbits make excellent pets—there's no doubt about it. They are easy to care for, they're interesting and entertaining, and they can even be trained. But like all living things, they have certain requirements that must be met in order to keep them happy and healthy. So can you meet the physical and emotional needs of a rabbit?

PHYSICAL CHARACTERISTICS

A rabbit's physical characteristics may qualify him for an adorability award, but they also reveal something about his needs. Knowing what kind of care a rabbit demands will make it easier for you to decide if a rabbit will fit into your lifestyle.

EARS: Rabbits obviously have an excellent sense of hearing, thanks to their radarlike ears. Large ears have a distinct advantage in the wild, where rabbits need to detect predators in plenty of time to escape, but they can cause some problems for domestic rabbits. Rabbits are known to be sensitive to the high-frequency emissions from televisions and microwaves, so it is best not to locate a rabbit cage next to these devices.

It is also tempting to use these lengthy appendages as a handle for picking up a rabbit, but regardless of how many times you've seen a magician retrieve a rabbit from his hat this way, that is not an appropriate way to handle a rabbit! Children,

especially, should be taught to refrain from handling their pet's ears in this manner.

TEETH: If the ears are a rabbit's most prominent feature, its teeth would come in a close second. The long incisor teeth sometimes cause people to mistake rabbits for rodents, but the rabbit's teeth actually have one very distinct difference from those of rodents. While mice, hamsters, and gerbils have two upper and two lower incisors, rabbits have four upper incisors—two of them hidden behind the front two. This is just one of the differences that have earned rabbits their own separate order, called *lagomorpha*, which includes both rabbits and hares. Even so, the rabbit's teeth do share at least one very important characteristic with the teeth of rodents: They never stop growing.

The rabbit's teeth grow continuously in order to compensate for the wear of constant gnawing. Rabbits require a constant source of chewing materials, and they must be watched carefully when outside their cages to be sure they do not chew on anything hazardous. Precautions need to be taken to cover electrical cords and block off dangerous areas when a rabbit is allowed to play on the floor.

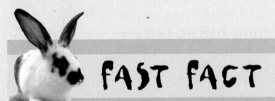

FAST FACT

Long ears are great for detecting sound, but they also have another job. Their large amount of skin surface and ample blood supply help regulate the rabbit's body temperature.

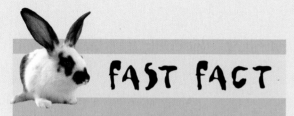

FAST FACT

A rabbit can live up to 10 years. Are you ready to make this kind of long-term commitment?

SIZE: Size is another characteristic to consider when deciding if a rabbit is a good choice of pet for you. The giant rabbit breeds, which can reach up to 16 pounds (7.3 kg), obviously require more room than smaller breeds. This translates into a greater investment in housing and more time spent on cage cleaning. You can also expect greater feed and supply expenses. Do you want the big responsibilities of a big bunny? Some people think a dog-sized bunny is worth the extra effort.

Smaller breeds have their own drawbacks. A petite dwarf may not be the best choice of pet for children, as the risk of being injured is so much greater for a diminutive bunny. They are also more apt to be harassed by other pets who think they are the perfect size to prey on. But miniaturized bunnies can be excellent companions for mature handlers who have the right living conditions to offer them.

Fortunately, there are also plenty of medium-sized rabbits that make

perfect pets for those who are not interested in size extremes. If you want a "rabbit-sized" rabbit, there are certainly many breeds in this category to choose from.

HAIR TYPES: Regardless of size, most rabbits are self-cleaning and require very little grooming—except for the long-haired breeds. Angora rabbits are the high-maintenance divas of the rabbit world. If you love fluff, you should be prepared to spend several hours every week grooming your pet. If you think you can minimize your workload by getting a smaller model, you'll be disappointed to learn they require just as much work as the larger angoras!

In addition to regular brushing, you'll have to keep your angora's cage exceptionally clean to avoid soiling and matting his coat. Angoras kept outdoors are more comfortable if they are clipped for the summer. If you have no interest in becoming a bunny barber, you may want to bypass the angora breeds.

There are a few longer-haired breeds that are slightly easier to maintain than the angoras. If you really go for the fuzzy look, the Jersey Wooly and the American Fuzzy Lop are good considerations. The Jersey Wooly has a hair length comparable to some of the angora breeds, but the abundance of guard hairs in its coat makes it much less prone to matting. The American Fuzzy Lop offers plenty of puffiness to cuddle, but has a somewhat shorter coat than the angoras, which is 2 inches (5 cm) in length compared to 3 to 5 inches (7.6–13 cm).

Short-haired rabbits are much easier to maintain, but that does not mean they come without hair concerns. Rabbits "molt," or shed their hair, twice or more a year. Regular brushing during these periods can minimize the hair in your home. If anyone in your household suffers from allergies, make sure a rabbit will be compatible with your situation before you bring one home.

LEGS AND FEET: When considering a rabbit as a pet, you also need to realize that a rabbit's long hind legs are designed to cover ground quickly. These legs are exceptionally strong and can injure small children or smaller pets. They also make it possible for a rabbit to kick out of your grasp quite easily, so you should learn how to hold a rabbit properly to avoid its injury or escape. It's always a good idea to teach your rabbit to tolerate handling so you can avoid

Teach everyone in your home the proper way to hold your rabbit to ensure his safety.

physical conflicts between you and your furry companion. (See Chapter 7 for ways to train your bunny.)

The biggest problem with a struggling rabbit is the scratches he leaves behind. These can be quite severe if the rabbit's nails have grown long and sharp. Domestic rabbits do not have the same opportunities as wild rabbits to wear down their nails, so they do need to be clipped occasionally. Are you willing to do this?

TEMPERAMENTAL CHARACTERISTICS

Rabbits also have their own emotional lives. Understanding how a rabbit thinks and what he thinks about can shed an enormous amount of light on your rabbit's behavior. Why does a rabbit "freeze" when he gets scared? Why is it possible to litter box train a rabbit? Why are rabbits such fastidious groomers?

A little bit of education in rabbit psychology will help you understand why your rabbit behaves the way he does, and what you need to do to meet your pet's emotional needs.

SOCIAL ANIMALS: Rabbits are social animals, which is one of the reasons they enjoy the company of humans and make such nice pets. It also explains why rabbits sometimes develop very close relationships with other animals, such as Guinea pigs, cats, and even dogs.

In the wild, groups of rabbits live in warrens, which are networks of burrows and tunnels. Like other social animals, rabbits establish a hierarchy and they are very communicative. A rabbit will let you know quite obviously when he likes or doesn't like something. Besides their clear body language, rabbits use various vocalizations that include squeals of excitement, purrs of contentment, and growls of aggression. Developing a mutually enjoyable relationship with your rabbit involves listening and responding to your pet's communication signals.

The flip side of sociability is loneliness. If your rabbit will be left home alone most of the day, you might want to consider getting more than one rabbit so your bunny has a

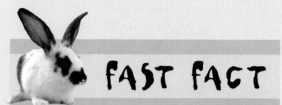

FAST FACT

A rabbit requires 5–10 minutes per day for feeding, 10–15 minutes every other day for cage cleaning, and at least 2–3 hours every day for out-of-cage playtime (of which 30 minutes should consist of human interaction).

buddy. Although this doubles the initial expenses of rabbit keeping, there is not much difference in the amount of time and effort necessary to care for two rabbits as opposed to one.

PREY ANIMALS: Rabbits occupy a place at the bottom of the food chain, and like other prey animals, they can be skittish when confronted by loud noises or sudden movements. A rabbit that is startled will either "freeze" or scurry for safety. Some rabbits can literally be "scared to death" when intense fear causes them to suffer cardiac arrest. The "fear factor" of the rabbit's psyche can cause considerable stress for a rabbit that is kept in the wrong environment.

What is the wrong environment? That depends entirely on the individual rabbit's demeanor. Domestication has left some rabbits with their wild ancestors' spirit fully intact. These bunnies have a well-developed flight response and are very reactive to their surroundings. Other rabbits have had this sensitivity dulled by the process of selective breeding. These guys can tolerate some noise and activity without flinching. But, for the most part, rabbits prefer a quieter environment and don't appreciate being harassed by a pet dog or boisterous children.

A nest box is an absolute necessity for a bunny, so he can retreat to a safe haven when things make him nervous or scared. And if you plan to show your bunny, he will benefit greatly from plenty of exposure to handling, traveling, and new environments at a young age so he can tolerate these things without too much stress as an adult.

PROLIFIC BREEDERS: One of rabbits' most notorious qualities is their ability to reproduce quickly and in great numbers. This is nature's way of providing an ample food supply for predators and ensuring the survival of the rabbit species. But this trait requires rabbit-keepers to be extremely diligent in controlling reproduction. You can quickly get buried in bunnies if you allow a buck (male rabbit) and doe (female rabbit) to breed indiscriminately! Rabbits kept as house pets are best off being neutered or spayed, and this can add a considerable expense to rabbit ownership. The benefits, however, are tremendous.

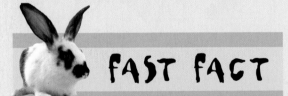

FAST FACT

Rabbits are most active in the morning and the evening—a perfect schedule for busy pet owners!

Without supervision, rabbits can multiply quickly. Be sure to keep non-neutered male rabbits separate from females!

Neutered bucks are less likely to spray urine in the home or become aggressive. Spayed rabbits pay more attention to their owners instead of preparing nests for future litters. Eliminating hormonally driven behaviors produces better-behaved bunnies.

RABBITS AND CHILDREN: The main components of a mutually happy relationship between children and rabbits are parental guidance, supervision, and intervention. A child should never be expected to take on complete responsibility for a pet, as the pet is sure to become neglected when the novelty wears off. This doesn't mean a child can't take care of her own pet; it just means that some parental supervision is necessary to make sure that the pet care duties are performed consistently. If

you don't want to assume these duties yourself, be prepared to do some prodding!

Rabbits do make delightful pets for children, but the duties expected of a child and the type of pet handling you allow should be age-appropriate. Children under the age of six or seven may have difficulty handling a rabbit properly, and they aren't always aware that their actions can cause pain to other creatures. The result can be injuries to the rabbit or the child.

You can avoid problems by enforcing rules and limits from the very beginning. Establish guidelines as to when and how often the child can interact with the rabbit. Decide what types of interactions will be allowed for younger children. And be sure to teach all children the proper

Children are often fascinated by small pets like rabbits. However, never allow young children to hold or play with a rabbit unsupervised.

way to pick up and hold a rabbit. Rabbits that become stressed and exhausted from improper handling are more prone to develop problems with biting and kicking.

RABBITS AND OTHER PETS: Humans are not the only creatures that enjoy interspecies relationships. Even seemingly "unnatural" relationships have developed between carnivores and prey, like dogs and horses or cats and rabbits. In all these cases, individual personality plays a huge part in the success of these friendships.

One dog might take his prey instincts a little too seriously and want nothing more to do with a rabbit than make a meal out of him. Another dog might think a rabbit makes an interesting playmate or cuddle buddy. Chances for success are greatest when the dog has a calm temperament and a low prey drive, and the rabbit is not too high-strung.

Better yet, if they are raised together, they are less likely to view each other as predator and prey.

Keep one thing in mind, however: If there is a conflict between a dog and a rabbit, the dog is more likely to win. For this reason, it is always best to take precautions to ensure your rabbit's safety. If there appears to be a great deal of tension between a dog and a rabbit, it is best to find a new home for the bunny. Being constantly harassed or "stared down" by a dog is a terrifying existence for a rabbit.

Cats tend to present fewer problems, as most rabbits are too big for them to seriously consider stalking

and preying on. Still, it's a good idea to take precautions to ensure your rabbit's safety until you've had a chance to see how your cat will react to his new housemate.

In general, a much more compatible companion for a rabbit is a Guinea pig. Guinea pigs have lifestyles similar to those of rabbits, which explains why these two species tend to get along so famously. Since they both eat similar food and require similar types of housing and supplies, it's quite easy to combine rabbit-keeping with Guinea pig-keeping. Even so, a rabbit and a Guinea pig can get into spats over

Rabbits can co-exist with your other household pets.

food or dominance, and the smaller Guinea pig may get the short end of it. So Guinea pigs and rabbits should be supervised when they are together, and they should have their own separate living quarters.

THE BEST ENVIRONMENT FOR A RABBIT

Unless you plan to breed rabbits for commercial or show purposes, the best place for a rabbit is in your home. Rabbits are social animals that appreciate interacting with their human and animal housemates. They need these interactions in order to maintain their tameness and to develop relationships.

If you are only interested in keeping a rabbit as an outdoor pet, you should evaluate your reasons for getting a rabbit. Do you really want a pet that you only see at feeding time? Do you want to forgo the opportunity to observe your pet more closely and be entertained by your "funny bunny"? You also need to consider that outdoor rabbits are more susceptible to illness, parasites, and predation. They are more prone to neglect, as it is easy to forget about a pet that lives apart from its human companions. Also, rabbits kept outdoors don't develop the strong bonds with their owners that make rabbit ownership so rewarding. Still insist on keeping your pet outdoors? Find him a bunny companion so he will not be so bored and lonely.

If you decide to keep your bunny indoors, he will become a true member of your family. Whether or not your home makes a good environment for a bunny depends somewhat on the individual rabbit. Some rabbits are great with younger children and actually thrive in an active, bustling household. Other rabbits become stressed by too much activity. As long as you are choosy in picking the right rabbit, there is sure to be a rabbit, somewhere, that will make a great addition to your family!

Even when a rabbit is kept indoors, it is difficult for him to truly blossom into a great companion if he's kept in a cage all day long. It's not good for his health to be confined to such a small space all the time, either. Rabbits need exercise. They like the mental stimulation that

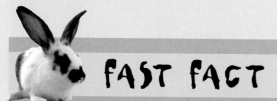

FAST FACT

Rabbits enjoy routine. They look forward to eating, playing, and interacting with their humans on a regular schedule. Can you provide this consistency for your furry pet?

comes from playing and exploring. Rabbits are happiest when they have a larger area, such as a safe room or pen, in which to hop around occasionally. Rabbits that are litter box trained may actually be given free run of the house, but only when their owners are home to supervise them.

RESPONSIBLE RABBIT OWNERSHIP

Choosing to bring a long-eared friend into your life involves more than making a commitment to care for a pet responsibly. It also means making a commitment to your friends, relatives, neighbors, and community to be a responsible pet owner. One of these responsibilities is to always keep control of your pet.

Allowing your rabbit to forage loose in your yard is not only dangerous for your rabbit, which might get lost or be attacked by a predator, but it is also ill-appreciated by neighbors, who may become understandably irate when your rabbit—with his voracious appetite for greenery—decimates their flower gardens. Always keep your rabbit under control and take precautions to prevent his escape from the home or his hutch.

If you want to give your bunny some outdoor playtime, provide a secure pen. There are even leashes designed for rabbits that allow you to

keep your pet under control and also give you a way to pick up your rabbit at any sign of danger. Some rabbits are also comfortable in harnesses designed for small dogs or cats. For extra protection, you should get your rabbit microchipped by your veterinarian.

A microchip is a tiny data chip that is injected under a rabbit's skin, just above the shoulders. If your rabbit accidentally gets lost—and this

You can walk your rabbit if he's on a leash or harness.

can happen even when you take the most stringent precautions—shelters, veterinarians, and animal control officers will be able to scan your pet for ownership information. Without a microchip, it is almost impossible to reunite a lost bunny with his owner.

Being respectful of others also applies inside your home. You know your bunny is the cutest, most endearing creature on the planet, but some of your guests may not be so enamored with your furry friend. Always ask people's permission before introducing them to your pet. As silly as it sounds, there are some people who are deathly afraid of rabbits!

Different communities also tend to have different perceptions of rabbits. Some rural communities consider rabbits as livestock, while more urban areas treat them like pets. In either case, the community's senti-

ments about rabbits are usually reflected in its ordinances. There may be regulations regarding the breeding or keeping of rabbits, whether indoors or out, and it is your responsibility to find out what kind of laws apply to rabbit-keeping in your area. The purpose of these laws is to protect animal welfare and individual rights, so you and your pet must obey them.

Even if there are no laws regarding rabbit reproduction, you should be aware that pet overpopulation has reached epidemic proportions. Rabbits, which are extremely prolific, face the same problem as dogs and cats—there are not enough homes for all of them. As a responsible pet owner, you need to take this problem seriously and take steps to control your rabbit's reproductive capabilities. Separate the sexes or

BEGINNING EXPENSES FOR RABBIT KEEPING

Rabbit	$20–$50	Toys	$10–$20
Outdoor hutch	$80–$120	Grooming supplies	$10–$20
Indoor cage	$40–$60	Nest box	$8–$12
Bedding	$8–$12	Pet carrier	$20–$30
Food and supplies	$20–$30	Neutering or spaying	$100–250

TOTAL $316–$604

Pet rabbits require a serious time commitment. As a rabbit owner, you'll have to feed your pet, clean his cage, and most importantly, spend time playing with him. Rabbits are social animals, and they thrive on attention and care.

have your pets neutered or spayed. On the plus side, having your rabbit surgically sterilized makes it easier to litter train him.

❧❧❧❧

Domestic rabbits rely entirely on humans for all their needs. Choosing to be a caregiver for another living creature is an awesome responsibility, but the rewards are priceless. There is no other experience that can teach us so much about life and relationships.

CHAPTER TWO

Rabbit History and Breeds

It may be hard to believe, but all domestic rabbits, in their great variety of sizes and colors, come from the same European ancestors. Although rabbits existed throughout Europe as far back as the early Pleistocene period, the climactic changes of the Ice Age pushed rabbit populations south, where they settled in what is now Spain and the Iberian Peninsula, and northwestern Africa.

Rabbits eventually repopulated much of Europe with the help of humans. As prolific and adaptable animals, their value as a food source was exploited by the Romans and early explorers, who captured them and released them into new territories to reproduce so they could be

Some types of rabbit, like the eastern cottontail, do not make good pets.

hunted for food. Thus, wild rabbits were eventually reestablished throughout much of Europe by the 13th century. At some point during their redistribution, these wild ancestors became domesticated.

The wild rabbit species that was to become our meat-producers, pelt-producers, and, eventually, our beloved pets, was *Oryctolagus cuniculus*. *Oryctolagus* is a Greek word that means "burrowing hare," and *cuniculus* is a Latin word that refers to the rabbit's subterranean lifestyle. The domesticated version of this species is now called *Oryctolagus cuniculus forma domestica*.

Oryctolagus cuniculus did not exist in the Americas, so all the domestic rabbits in the United States originated from European stock. The wild cottontails that are indigenous to the Americas are untamable and do not thrive in captivity. Attempts to domesticate them, as well as attempts to domesticate other species of wild rabbits and hares, have not been successful.

"RABBIT PLAGUES"

Along with the purposeful release of rabbits into new territories, it was inevitable that some captive rabbits would escape into new areas to which they had been brought. Unfortunately, the ecosystems in some of these new lands could not always handle the rabbit's prolific and destructive tendencies. Without predators or diseases to keep their populations in check, rabbits reproduced unabated and caused "rabbit plagues."

One of the greatest of these occurred in Australia after a number of rabbits were either released or escaped around 1860. The rabbit population explosion that ensued caused so much damage to crops and vegetation that drastic measures had to be taken to control it. A viral disease, called myxomatosis, was developed and released into the wild rabbit population.

While this seriously curbed rabbit populations in Australia, there were some dire consequences. The disease subsequently found its way into the wild rabbit populations of Europe, perhaps being transported there by fleas or mosquitoes on trade vessels. From wild rabbits, the disease was easily passed to domestic rabbits that are housed outdoors, and it continues to be a concern for rabbit breeders in Europe. Fortunately, the impact of myxomatosis on domestic rabbits in the United States is limited, perhaps because the wild rabbit species in this country—which would provide the means of spreading it—are not susceptible to it. Meanwhile, the wild rabbits in Australia have progressively developed some immunity to the disease, and their numbers have again reached "pest" status.

RABBITS VERSUS HARES

Rabbits and hares appear to have a lot in common, but there are actually significant differences between them. Some rabbits even look quite a bit like hares, with the same long ears and lean, well-arched bodies. At least one domestic rabbit breed is named after hares: the Belgian Hare. But none of our domestic rabbit breeds is a hare. In fact, hares have never been tamed and they are incapable of interbreeding with rabbits.

The hare's offspring are born with fur and open eyes, while rabbit offspring are born hairless, blind and helpless. Even the behavior patterns of hares are different from those of rabbits. Hares live solitary lives, unlike rabbits, which are more social. Hares' nests are constructed aboveground rather than belowground, and their precocious young are capable of leaving the nest quite early.

DEVELOPMENT OF RABBIT BREEDS

The harelike body type of some rabbit breeds is just one of five different body types that have been developed in domestic rabbits. A rainbow of colors, a diverse palette of patterns, and an assortment of sizes have also evolved, most of them emerging just in the last century. Some came about through selective breeding in the pursuit of better meat producers, some were bred to produce superior pelts or wool, and some were developed for multiple purposes.

BODY TYPES: The domestic rabbit's hunched body posture has been refined and exaggerated in various

This rabbit has a compact body style, creating the most familiar rabbit silhouette.

COLORS WITHIN GROUPS

The following are some of the colors within the various color groups:

Chinchilla
Lilac
Squirrel
Lynx
Opal
Pearl

Smoke pearl
Black
Blue
Chocolate
Sable
Seal

Tortoiseshell
Fawn
Red
Steel
Cream

breeds to create several distinct types. The semi-arched rabbit has the squatting posture that most would associate with a natural rabbit shape. The compact type is a short-bodied version consistent with smaller rabbits and the dwarf breeds. The full-arch type has a more alert, upright posture that resembles the stance of a hare. The commercial type applies to meat-type rabbits that are larger and fleshier. And the cylindrical type, as its name suggests, is long and slender (the only breed that belongs to this group is the Himalayan).

COLOR GROUPS AND VARIETIES:

The most exciting developments in domestic rabbits are the great variety of colors and markings. Some rabbit breeds are known for their distinctive colors or markings, while other breeds offer an array of choices.

Breed standards define the acceptable color groups and varieties for each breed.

One of the most common patterns is a self-colored animal, which bears the same color over its entire body, head, and extremities. A pure black rabbit would be a good example.

This black lop is a prime example of a self-colored rabbit.

The agouti variety most closely resembles the color characteristics of wild rabbits, with three or more bands of color on each hair shaft. Instead of being limited to the standard wild-gray agouti color, however, domestic rabbits come in a number of attractive agouti hues.

Broken varieties combine white with areas of color. Because they are so visually appealing, broken varieties are a popular choice for pets. A pointed white rabbit is mostly white with a colored nose, ears, feet, legs, and tail. The color of the "points" depends on the breed.

Shaded rabbits have a darker color on the back, head, ears, tail, and legs that gradually fades into a lighter color on the other areas of the body. The contrast in shaded rabbits is softer than in other color patterns, but they are no less attractive. Finally, rabbits whose guard hairs are a different color from the surface color or undercolor are called ticked. Ticking often has the effect of making the coat look deeper.

One of the most distinctive color patterns is the tan pattern, which is characterized by a contrasting color on the eye circles, nostrils, chest, belly, inside of the legs, underside of the tail, and inside edge of the ears. The contrasting color depends on the

TERMS RELATING TO A RABBIT'S HAIR

Banding—A hair shaft that has bands of two or more colors.

Base color—The fur color closest to the skin; also called undercolor.

Brindling—The intermixing of two different colors of hair.

Butterfly—A butterfly-shaped marking over the nose and front of the face.

Flyback—When hair that is stroked against its natural direction of growth returns to its normal position.

Guard hair—Protective hair that is longer and has thicker, stiffer shafts than the undercoat.

Points—The ears, nose, tail, feet and legs.

Surface color—The visible surface color of the hair; in some cases, the color of the hair tips.

Ticking—When the guard hairs are a different color than the rest of the coat.

color on the rest of the rabbit's body, but don't let the name fool you—tan-pattern rabbits do not always have tan markings. The wide band color group also requires a specific distribution of colors, but without as much contrast as the tan pattern. Most of the head, body, and extremities of those designated as wide band must all be the same color, with a lighter shade allowed on the eye circles, inside the ears, on the jowls, and on the belly.

BREEDS

Most rabbit breeds were bred for reasons other than temperament; yet, almost any breed of rabbit can make a good pet. Why? Because all rabbits are naturally sweet-natured! The following are some of the most popular breeds for show or as pets:

AMERICAN: The American is a solid-colored rabbit that comes in two specific colors: blue and white. This breed is most popular in—you guessed it—America. Blue Americans have blue-gray eyes, and white Americans have pink eyes. This is a medium-sized rabbit, about 9–12 pounds (4–5.5 kg), with a uniform shade of color over its entire body. Any shading of the color, or patches of foreign colors, would be disqualifications for a show rabbit.

AMERICAN SABLE: The American Sable's greatest asset is its rich, shaded brown color, which gives it a warm, soft appearance. Its brown eyes have a unique ruby-red glow. Show rabbits are required to have very specific shading, and rabbits that lack the red glow of the eyes are disqualified. This medium-sized rabbit weighs in at 7–10 pounds (3.2–4.5 kg).

THE ANGORAS: Like other angora breeds, the English Angora looks much larger than it actually is, due to its fluffy fur, which can grow up to 5 inches (13 cm) long. At 5–7 pounds (2.2–3.2 kg), this is a medium-small rabbit. It normally

For spectacularly soft fur, it is impossible to beat the angora.

carries its ears in a distinctive "V" shape, with pronounced feathering and tassels on the ears. A great deal of attention is devoted to the show rabbit's coat, which should have a uniform length and density over the entire body.

The French Angora does not have the heavily furred ears of the English Angora, although some tufting on the tips is allowed for show rabbits. It also has shorter hair, which reaches up to 3.5 inches (9 cm) in length. This angora is only slightly larger, with an average weight of 8 pounds (3.6 kg).

The largest of this breed is the Giant Angora. Technically, there is no limit to a Giant Angora's weight, as breed standards do not specify a maximum size, but they usually average between 10 and 12 pounds (4.5–5.5 kg). With hair that is ideally 4 inches (10 cm) long, they appear quite large indeed. One of the unique features of the Giant Angora is that its coat contains three fiber types. In addition to the underwool and guard hair typical of other angoras, there is an "awn fluff," which is longer and wavier than the underwool, and has tips that resemble guard hair. The Giant Angora sports well-tasseled ears that are held in the typical angora "V" shape. Due to the production of so much hair, this breed does better on a higher-protein diet than other rabbits do. A wire-bottom cage can help keep feces from soiling the Giant Angora's coat. This high-maintenance breed is for the serious rabbit fancier only.

The Satin Angora has its own unique characteristic—an unusual sheen to its coat, which is caused by the translucent quality of its hair shafts. This medium-sized angora breed runs 6.5 to 9 pounds (3–4 kg), with hair that grows approximately 3 inches (7.6 cm) long. The Satin Angora carries its ears erect, instead of in a "V," and the ears may or may not have small tufts of hair on the tips. All the angora breeds come in a huge variety of colors.

BELGIAN HARE: The Belgian Hare looks much like one would expect a hare-type rabbit to look: leggy and streamlined. Its lean body, which reaches an average of 8 pounds (3.6

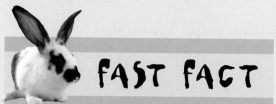

FAST FACT

Rabbits were originally classified as rodents in the order *rodentia*. It wasn't until 1945 when the case was made to put rabbits into their own order called *lagomorpha*.

kg), gives this rabbit the appearance of speed and athleticism. Its stiff-textured fur comes in a deep-red color with a slate-blue undercolor.

BEVEREN: The Beveren is a wonderful example of a fur breed, whose dense and highly textured coat is held in high esteem. Growing to an average length of 1.5 inches (3.8 cm), the Beveren's fur comes in three colors: black, blue, and white. A great deal of importance is also placed on the length of the show rabbit's ears, which should ideally be 5 inches (13 cm) long. Beverens with ears less than 4.75 inches (12 cm) long are disqualified. This breed comes in a versatile size range between 8 and 11 pounds (3.6–5 kg).

BRITANNIA PETITE: As its name suggests, the Britannia Petite is a miniaturized rabbit with a maximum weight of 2.5 pounds (1.1 kg). Unlike the more popular Netherland Dwarf, the Britannia Petite does not have short ears and a

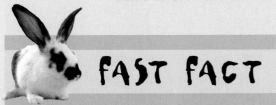

FAST FACT

In the majority of rabbit breeds, females tend to be larger than males.

cobby head, but instead, looks more like a full-sized rabbit in a small body. Its fur comes in several colors: black, black otter (black body with white or cream belly), chestnut agouti, ruby-eyed white, and sable marten. This sprightly breed may be temperamental.

CALIFORNIAN: The Californian has attractive markings that resemble those of a Siamese cat. The dark color of the nose, ears, feet, and tail should be as close to black as possible, while the remainder of the body should be a pure, unblemished white. This rabbit comes in a solidly proportioned body that reaches anywhere from 8 to 10.5 pounds (3.6–4.7 kg).

CHECKERED GIANT: Like the many other giant breeds, the breed standard for the Checkered Giant does not specify a maximum size, but it requires a minimum size of 11 pounds (5 kg) for bucks and 12 pounds (5.5 kg) for does. With a well-arched body, the Checkered Giant shows plenty of "daylight underneath," according to the standard, as it carries its body off the ground. This rabbit is easy to recognize by the very distinctive markings on its white coat. These markings may be either black or blue, and they consist of a stripe down the spine, eye circles, a butterfly pattern over the nose, a single spot on each cheek, and two spots on each side of the hindquarters.

THE CHINCHILLAS: The Chinchilla breeds are distinguished by their beautiful chinchilla color, which consists of a dark slate-blue base color, a pearl color in the middle of the hair shaft, and a small band of black near the tip. The coat is ticked with jet-black hair that makes it look identical to chinchilla fur. The American Chinchilla is a medium-sized rabbit, weighing in at 9–12 pounds (4–5.5 kg). The Giant Chinchilla's impressive physique tips the scales at 12–16 pounds (5.5–7.3 kg). And the more petite Standard Chinchilla is a modest 5–7.5 pounds (2.2–3.4 kg).

DUTCH: One of the most common pet rabbits due to its smaller size—about 4.5 pounds (2 kg)—and amiable personality, the Dutch rabbit is easy to recognize by its coat pattern. The rear feet are white, and the front half of its body is white, except for

A litter of baby chinchilla rabbits. American chinchillas are good breeders, with an average litter of seven to ten kits.

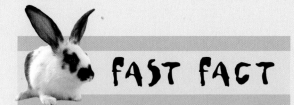

the sides of the face and the ears. This leaves an attractive white blaze down the front of the face. The colored portions of this rabbit can be one of a number of colors, including black, blue, chocolate, gray, steel, and tortoiseshell.

ENGLISH SPOT: The most prominent feature of the English Spot is its striking color pattern. This predominantly white rabbit has solid coloring on the nose, ears, and eye rings. A solid stripe runs down its back, and a "chain" of spots decorates its sides. The colored portions of this rabbit can be any one of a number of colors, including black, blue, chocolate, gold, gray, lilac, or tortoiseshell. The English Spot comes in a manageable smaller size of 5–8 pounds (2.2–3.6 kg), which makes it a practical choice for a pet.

FLEMISH GIANT: The Flemish Giant grows to a minimum of 13 pounds (5.9 kg) and 20 inches (51 cm) long. These massive representatives of the rabbit species have well-proportioned physical characteristics for their size, and come in a variety of colors that include black, blue, fawn, light gray, sandy, steel gray, and white. If you want a rabbit that will make a very "big" impression, the Flemish Giant is definitely up to the task. Just keep in mind that this Great Dane of rabbits requires plenty of room!

FLORIDA WHITE: In case you haven't guessed it, the Florida White is a pure white specimen. This breed falls on the small end of the size scale at 4–6 pounds (1.8–2.7 kg). It was originally developed for research use, but its adorably cute looks have made it quite appealing to pet owners.

HARLEQUIN: There are two Harlequin varieties—the Japanese and the Magpie—and both are equally attractive. Although both possess striking color patterns that include alternating patches or bands of color on the body, the Magpie includes the color white and the Japanese does not. Perhaps the most interesting marking is the division of colors on the face, with half the face in one color and the other half in another color. Each Harlequin variety comes in four different color combinations and reaches a medium-small size of 6.4 to 9.5 pounds (2.9–4.3 kg).

HIMALAYAN: The Himalayan is easily recognized by the unique color points on its nose, ears, feet, and tail. In contrast to its white body, these color points can come in black, blue, chocolate, and lilac. The Himalayan is a long, lean breed that falls into the small category at approximately 3.5 pounds (1.6 kg). A very popular companion bunny!

HOTOT: The Hotot is distinguished by its specific color pattern. This rabbit is pure white, except for very prominent black bands around the eyes. Its coat has a distinctive sheen, caused by a profusion of longer guard hairs. Bred for its lush fur, the Hotot runs 8–11 pounds (3.6–5 kg), but the Dwarf Hotot has the same features in a miniature size. Reaching a maximum weight of 3 pounds (1.4 kg), the Dwarf Hotot has the same compact body and adorably small ears as other dwarf

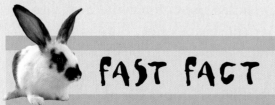

FAST FACT

Male rabbits have a scent gland under their chins. If you see your rabbit rubbing his chin on a favorite object, he is marking it with his scent.

rabbits, and makes for a delightful animal companion.

JERSEY WOOLY: As its name implies, the Jersey Wooly is a fuzzy-looking member of the rabbit family, but it is generally not used for commercial wool production. Even though its hair grows to about 3 inches (7.6 cm), it is considered easier to care for than some of the angora breeds because of the qualities of its hair. In addition to being slightly lower maintenance, its fluffy coat comes in a great variety of colors in almost all the color groups. Its smaller size, at about 3 pounds (1.4 kg), and its short-eared cute looks make it one of the most desirable of the long-haired breeds for a pet.

THE LOPS: Perhaps the most recognizable of the rabbit breeds are lops, with their droopy ears and puppy-dog looks. One of the most notable of these is the English Lop, which has the largest, floppiest ears of them all. For show purposes, these ears must measure at least 21 inches (53 cm) from the tip of one ear to the tip of the other ear. The width of the ear is also taken into consideration, with the widest point expected to be about one-quarter the length of the ear. The ears aren't the only large part of this rabbit, as it reaches a minimum of 9 pounds (4 kg) for adult bucks and 10 pounds (4.5 kg) for adult does.

The French Lop is also a sizable rabbit at 10 pounds (4.7 kg) and over. This thickly constructed lop breed has floppy ears that reach at least 1.25 inches (3.2 cm) below its jaw, which means they are often touching the ground. French Lops come in six different color groups—agouti, broken, self, shaded, ticked and wide band.

The Mini Lop is a popular pet lop breed due to its smaller size of 4.5 to 6.5 pounds (2–2.9 kg). Its wide array of colors and patterns offer much to choose from, and its thick construction makes it a very sturdy rabbit.

The Holland Lop is also a popular pet variety. With an ideal weight of 3 pounds (1.4 kg) and a huge variety of

This Holland Lop is distinguished by its long, floppy ears.

colors and patterns, there is probably a Holland Lop somewhere that can please the most choosy of pet owners.

The American Fuzzy Lop has a lot of "stuffed animal" appeal. Although lop-eared rabbits are an old breed, the American Fuzzy Lop is relatively new, first recognized as a breed by the ARBA in 1988. These are smaller rabbits, which run from 3 to 4 pounds (1.4–1.8 kg) as adults. Temperamentally, they tend to be a little high-strung. Their 2-inch (5 cm) long coat does require more maintenance than those of other lops to keep it clean and looking its best. Like the other lops, it comes in a wide array of colors from almost all the different color groups (except ticked and tan pattern).

The cute little Netherland Dwarf is a popular pet.

NETHERLAND DWARF: If rabbits were judged on cuteness alone, the miniature Netherland Dwarf would definitely take the prize. With an average adult weight of 2 pounds (1 kg), along with its short ears and round head, the Netherland Dwarf never loses its "baby bunny" appearance. Add these features to an abundance of color varieties, and it's clear to see why the Netherland Dwarf has become such a popular pet. But its small size demands mature handling, and it is not a good pet for small children.

NEW ZEALAND: The New Zealand is a rabbit of substance, developed for its value as a meat producer. It is perhaps best known as a large white rabbit, but it also comes in black and red. This sizable bunny, which runs 9–12 pounds (4–5.4 kg), is known to hold its own among other house pets, as it has plenty of weight to throw around.

REX: The Rex is a nice, medium-sized rabbit at 8–9 pounds (3.6–4 kg), best known for its short, high-density, easy-care hair. The Rex's hair is so dense that it literally stands upright, perpendicular to the body. This gives the coat a plush texture that is inviting to touch and pet. Without longer guard hairs to add coarseness to its coat, the Rex is said to have one of the softest coats in rabbitdom. In addition, the Rex offers many popular choices in colors and markings from several different color groups.

As if it didn't have enough going for it, the Rex also comes in a smaller 4 pound (1.8 kg) size called a Mini Rex. Both are exceptionally popular as pet breeds.

RHINELANDER: The Rhinelander has a well-arched body type and displays markings of both black and golden-orange on a white background. The markings include a spine stripe, a butterfly pattern on the face, spots on the sides and hindquarters, cheek spots, eye circles, and colored ears. An exceptionally attractive rabbit, the Rhinelander weighs in at 6.5 to 10 pounds (2.9–4.5 kg).

SATIN: The Satin possesses an unusual hair quality that gives its fur a distinctive sheen and makes its colors appear more intense. This "satin" effect is caused by a translucent hair shaft that reflects light. The Satin's hair shafts are also smaller in diameter than normal rabbit fur, which makes its fur softer to the touch. With ideal weights of 9.5 pounds (4.3 kg) for bucks and 10 pounds (4.5 kg) for does, this rabbit is on the large

The rex rabbit is known for its extremely soft fur. Rabbits of this breed are sometimes called "velveteen rabbits."

side. It comes in multiple color varieties in several different color groups.

THE SILVERS: A well-proportioned smaller rabbit is the Silver, which runs 4–7 pounds (1.8–3.2 kg). Contrary to its name, this rabbit isn't really a silver color. The name refers to "silvering," which is the even interspersion of white or white-tipped hairs throughout the coat. The Silver's base color may be black, brown, or fawn.

Similar to the Silver, the Silver Fox is distinguished by the "silvering" of its coat. This breed, however, is quite a bit larger at 9–12 pounds (4–5.5 kg), and it always has a base coat of black. Ideally, the degree of silvering should be balanced so that the Silver Fox does appear silver, rather than black or gray.

Another "silvered" breed, the Silver Marten displays silvering only on its sides and rump. It also sports a silver-white color on its nostrils, eye circles, and inside of the ears. This medium sized breed runs 6–9.5 pounds (2.7–4.3 kg) and comes in black, blue, chocolate, and sable.

TAN: The Tan is another breed with a misleading name. This breed is not completely tan—it comes in black, blue, chocolate, and lilac—but each of these colors carries tan markings. The tan pattern consists of a tan triangle formed between the base of the ears and the point of the shoulders; a tan chest, belly, and underside of the tail; tan eye circles, nostrils, and jowls; tan on the feet and legs; and tan brindling on the lower sides and rump. In addition to the unique color pattern offered by this breed, the fur of this 4–6 pound (1.8–2.7 kg) rabbit is known to be exceptionally glossy.

RABBIT ORGANIZATIONS

All these different breeds of rabbit would not be recognizable if they did not possess certain characteristics that distinguish them from one another. And it would be impossible to consistently maintain these characteristics if there weren't formal descriptions of them, called standards. Although animal shows had already become quite popular by the mid-1800s, it wasn't until the late 1800s that rabbit fanciers began to form clubs and draft the standards necessary to encourage uniformity in their breeds. Rabbit fanciers of the time also recognized the need for a larger, central organization to govern shows for all breeds of rabbits.

AMERICAN RABBIT BREEDERS ASSOCIATION (ARBA): The American Rabbit Breeders Association (ARBA) began in the

United States as the National Pet Stock Association in 1910. It managed shows for a number of small mammal species, including rabbits, cavies (Guinea pigs), and hamsters. The group changed its name to The American Rabbit and Cavy Breeders Association in 1923, and limited its scope of authority to rabbits and cavies alone. In 1952, the name was changed again, to its present designation, when cavy breeders decided to form their own national organization. Rabbit breeders and cavy breeders have since reunited into one overarching organization, but the name remains the ARBA.

The ARBA currently deals with almost 50 different breeds of rabbit and 13 different breeds of cavy. In addition to maintaining the standards for all these breeds and governing rabbit and cavy shows around the country, the ARBA gets involved in just about anything that affects

rabbit and cavy fanciers. It provides a variety of support services for its members, who include commercial producers, show fanciers, and pet owners. Its Web site, www.arba.net, is a valuable source of information for novice rabbit fanciers.

BRITISH RABBIT COUNCIL (BRC): The British Rabbit Council (BRC) governs rabbit shows in the United Kingdom and deals with issues that affect rabbit fanciers throughout Europe. Like the ARBA, the BRC also evolved and went through several name changes until it finally settled on the BRC in 1934. The BRC updates and produces a breed standard book periodically, which every serious rabbit fancier in the UK should possess. Its Web site, www.thebrc.org, provides links to many informative articles on rabbit care, breeding, and showing.

੬୬੬੬

Whether you seek an affectionate, easy-care pet, or an award-winning show rabbit, rabbit ownership offers a multitude of rewards. Just about any breed of rabbit can make a quiet, interactive, and entertaining pet if it is raised and handled properly. Have fun exploring and learning about the many different breeds of rabbit, so you can choose the ideal bunny companion for you and your family.

CHAPTER THREE

Finding the Right Rabbit

Searching for the perfect bunny can be just as much fun as treasure hunting! But how do you know when you've found the right one? If you have a clear idea about what you want before you go looking for it, you'll be sure to have a "Eureka!" moment.

Do you want a purebred rabbit you can show? Do you just want a fuzzy, long-eared companion? Do you need an exceptionally gentle bunny as a child's pet? Or do you want to play matchmaker for a bunny you already have? Perhaps you want your bunny to fill more than one of these roles. If you make a list of all the reasons you want a rabbit and the physical and temperamental characteristics that appeal to

Even rabbits from the same litter will exhibit very different personality traits.

you, you'll know what to watch for during your search.

CHOOSING A RABBIT

You may not find a rabbit that meets all your requirements, but don't compromise on the important stuff. A diamond in the rough is still a diamond, but fool's gold will never be worth much. What means the most to you?

TEMPERAMENT: Although all rabbits share some species-specific temperamental traits, such as a strong freeze-or-flight response to danger,

FAST FACT

When going to meet a prospective pet, always take some small bunny treats with you (carrots or broccoli are favorites) so you can entice the bunny to interact with you.

there is plenty of room for individuality as well. Some rabbits are known to be more high-strung or spirited than others. Some are lovely lap bunnies, and others prefer to be more active. Some tend to have a greater affinity for humans, while others prefer the company of other animals.

When evaluating a potential pet rabbit, watch how he responds to members of your family.

Evaluating individual rabbits can be difficult, since you may not have a lot of time to get to know your future pet, and you may not be able to see his reaction in various settings. But you can learn a lot through close observation. How does the rabbit respond to being handled by a stranger (you)? Does he seem skittish and afraid of people, or cautiously curious? Is he willing to take a piece of food out of your hand? Does he seem to be in perpetual motion, or does he lie around like king of the hutch? And don't forget to ask the owner or the shelter staff about the bunny's personality—they have known the animal much longer than you and can probably give you some valuable insights.

If you're getting a companion for a bunny you already have, your opinion isn't the only one that counts. Rabbits can be very choosy about their friends, so you'll need to "ask" your pet which personality traits he likes, too. This is usually accomplished by giving your pet a chance to meet potential bunny companions. Many bunny rescues are more than willing to arrange a "date" between rabbits. You can ask sellers if they will permit you to take a rabbit on a trial basis in case the relationship doesn't work out.

PHYSICAL CHARACTERISTICS:

Rabbits have little preference for the physical traits of their friends, but that doesn't mean these things shouldn't be important to you. You should already have a general idea of the physical characteristics that appeal to you. But do you know what conformation flaws might affect a rabbit's health? Look for a rabbit that has straight legs, a good posture, a balanced build, and well-aligned teeth. Rabbits that appear to have hereditary flaws on the outside are sure to have flaws on the inside as well.

Physical characteristics take on even more importance if you plan to show your rabbit. Rabbits are not judged on personality (although aggressive rabbits may be disqualified). To find a rabbit with the right physical attributes to impress the judges, you need to be an expert in rabbit conformation. Study the breed standard for the breed of your choice,

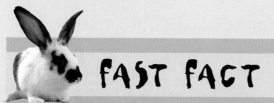

FAST FACT

Do not purchase a rabbit that is less than eight weeks old. Baby rabbits can suffer health problems if they are removed from their mothers sooner than this.

and don't be afraid to seek the opinions of experienced breeders before purchasing your first show rabbit.

MALE OR FEMALE

Both male and female rabbits make excellent pets, but there are certain situations when gender matters. If you plan to keep more than one rabbit, two bucks will disrupt your household harmony with conflicts that may become exceptionally violent. Two females will get along the best. You can also consider one of each sex if the male is neutered. For single-bunny households, you'll be happy to know that a rabbit of either sex can possess a delightful personality, especially when neutered or spayed.

HEALTH

While searching for the bunny of your dreams, you should know that it's very easy to mistake lethargy for a wonderfully calm temperament. If you think you've found the perfect pet rabbit because he doesn't flinch when you pick him up, and he remains quiet in your arms for an extended period, check to see if he's healthy. Rabbits are spirited creatures, and most of them would prefer to play on the floor than be held in your arms.

If a bunny sits bunched up with his fur ruffled out, that's a sign that he doesn't feel good. Any discharge from the eyes, nose, or mouth is an indication of illness. Patches of hair loss, scratching, or a bloated belly may be signs of parasites. No matter how perfectly sweet and docile a sick rabbit seems to be, you can be sure he is not displaying his true personality.

So don't take any chances by purchasing or adopting a sick bunny. In fact, any other bunnies at the same facility may have the same illness, even if they don't show symptoms yet. It's best to go elsewhere to find your new bunny. If you already have a bunny at home, you'll have to wash your hands and change your clothes after handling a sick bunny so you don't spread the illness to your own pet.

WHERE TO FIND A RABBIT

Now that you know what to look for, you're probably anxious to get on with the task of choosing a rabbit. You can't wait to go out and start meeting bunnies, talking to bunny people, and preparing for the addition of a new pet to your household. But where do you start? That depends on the type of rabbit you've decided to pursue.

Rabbits can be purchased from breeders and pet shops, or they can be adopted from shelters and rescue groups. They can even be located via the Internet. Each source provides certain types of rabbits and offers its own advantages and disadvantages.

SHELTER OR RESCUE: If you're interested in obtaining a fine pet and have no interest in showing or breeding rabbits, there are many homeless adult rabbits available at shelters and rescue organizations that can be adopted for reasonable fees. Even though many of the rabbits from these sources are mixed breeds, they may still possess many purebred characteristics that appeal to you. You will no doubt find a rainbow of colors, an assortment of sizes, a broad range of personalities, and a choice of erect or lop ears.

Some of the benefits of picking out your next fuzzy friend at a shelter or rescue include the cost, counseling, and ongoing support offered by these groups. Most shelters and rescues give their rabbits a clean bill of health before putting them up for adoption. Since veterinary costs are

You may find wonderful rabbits who desperately need new homes at a local animal shelter or a rescue organization.

often the most expensive part of acquiring a new pet, the cost savings can be significant. If you're not certain about the type of rabbit that might be appropriate for you, shelter or rescue staff can provide counseling to make sure the bunny you choose is a good match. These organizations are always more than willing to give you ongoing advice and support even after the adoption, which is a huge plus for first-time rabbit owners.

Homeless rabbits, however, do not always come with a complete history. It can be difficult to tell exactly how old they are, how they have been treated in the past, or what kind of behavior issues they may have developed. These drawbacks may have little impact on your decision if age and history are not important to you, and if behavior issues are minor and easily correctable. But if a rabbit has severe or perplexing behavior problems, which you do not feel qualified to handle, you are best off letting someone more experienced adopt the animal.

Listen to your better judgment and don't allow yourself to fall in love with an animal just because you feel sorry for it. While it is admirable to open your heart and home to a homeless animal, you still need to choose a pet that fits comfortably in your lifestyle.

Shelters and rescues are a great source of pet-quality rabbits, but beware of organizations that do not appear to be run professionally. Rescues, in particular, are often started by people who have good intentions but very little practical experience or knowledge of how to operate an animal welfare organization. Pay attention to the requirements in pet adoption contracts, as they can vary considerably from one organization to the next. If there is anything that makes you feel uncomfortable about an organization, seriously consider finding another source for your pet.

BREEDER: Breeders are a good source of purebred rabbits, whether you are interested in a pet, a show prospect, or breeding stock. The best place to find breeders is where breeders like to congregate—rabbit

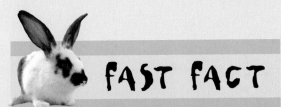

FAST FACT

It may seem burdensome to read the fine print on adoption contracts or purchase agreements, but it is very important to read them and thoroughly understand them. If something isn't clear to you, don't be afraid to ask about it.

shows. You can learn a lot about the hobby of rabbit showing and breeding by mingling with those who are more experienced, and at shows you'll certainly find rabbit fanciers who enjoy talking to you about their favorite breeds! Rabbit shows are a great place to learn, network, and perhaps find the bunny you've always wanted.

You can also locate breeders by contacting regional ARBA clubs listed on the ARBA Web site, www.arba.net. Belonging to a club, however, does not guarantee that a breeder is rep-

utable. This is something you'll have to determine by doing your own research. Always inspect a breeder's facilities before purchasing a rabbit from her, and pay attention to the cleanliness of the pens or cages. The quality of a rabbit's environment is often a good indication of the quality of its breeding.

Are the rabbits fearful of humans, or are they curious and friendly? Some breeders become overwhelmed with too many rabbits and don't have the time to handle and socialize all of them. Rabbits that have little

If you'd like a rabbit you can show, a breeder may be your best choice.

affinity for humans might make fine breeding stock, but they don't make the best pets. If you want an affectionate bunny, choose one that has received plenty of human attention and handling.

Reputable breeders are very concerned about producing quality animals, so they keep detailed records on their pedigrees and health. If you seek a bunny worthy of blue ribbons, you should expect nothing less than written documentation of your pet's lineage and other pertinent information. If a breeder can't locate this information or promises it at a "later date," don't wait for that date to arrive—take your business elsewhere.

When you choose your breeder wisely, she can become your mentor, your source of advice, maybe even your new best friend. A breeder can introduce you to the wonderful world of rabbit showing, direct you to a good rabbit vet, tell you where to

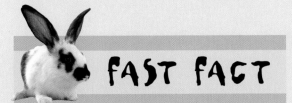

FAST FACT

A well-bred show prospect should come with a pedigree, which outlines the animal's ancestry. Reputable show breeders always keep meticulous records on their stock.

find good deals on rabbit supplies, and give you a few secret tips on show grooming. You're not just buying a show rabbit; you're forging a new human relationship, too!

PET SHOP: Bunnies can be found aplenty in pet shops, where their cages are often kept in pristine condition because they also function as point-of-purchase displays. (If the cages aren't clean, do a prompt about-face and take your business elsewhere!) The only problem to consider is this: What kind of environment did the bunny live in before the pet shop acquired him? It's anyone's guess as to where a pet shop gets its rabbit stock. Some pet shop rabbits come from commercial breeders (those who breed specifically for the pet shop trade). Some come from backyard breeders (pet owners who allowed their pets to reproduce). But regardless of the original source, you probably won't find any show prospects at the pet emporium.

Still, a pet shop rabbit can be just as lovable a pet as any other bunny. And you can't beat the convenience. A pet shop can be your one-stop bunny shop, since you can purchase all the supplies you need to get started in rabbit-keeping at the same place where you purchase your rabbit. Package deals are common, and they eliminate the possibility that you might forget something. But no matter how great a deal you might find here, you should still evaluate a rabbit carefully for health and personality.

Reputable pet shops will provide some kind of health guarantee and return policy in writing. Read these carefully! Some health guarantees don't really guarantee anything, and return policies can be overly restrictive. Make sure you understand all the provisions in any purchase contract, because it's not just your money on the line—it's your heart, too! It can take only a matter of hours to become totally enamored of your new pet, but it will take much longer to get over the grief of losing him. Pet shops that offer the best health and return policies have the most confidence in the quality of their stock.

THE INTERNET: One of the easiest ways to locate the right rabbit is to search the Internet. It can save you an enormous amount of time, gas, and effort. For adoptable rabbits, you can check the Web sites of local animal shelters for photos and descriptions of homeless bunnies. Better yet, you can visit the

You may be able to find your next rabbit friend just by "hopping" on the Internet. But it's always best to go see the bunnies before buying one, rather than purchasing sight unseen online.

Petfinder.com Web site, which hosts listings of adoptable rabbits throughout the country. You might even discover a nearby rabbit rescue organization you didn't know existed!

You can also use the Internet to locate rabbit breeders who might otherwise be difficult to find. Some breeders maintain their own Web sites and post announcements of litters, so you'll know when they have rabbits for sale. Corresponding over the Internet is convenient and inexpensive, and searching online provides more choices, more opportunities, and better chances of finding the right rabbit for you.

While the Internet is a great search tool, it should not be used as a method of commerce. Purchasing a rabbit isn't the same as buying a chair or a stereo system online. You don't need to worry about the breeding or temperament of a chair. You don't need to worry about the stress or trauma to a stereo system when it is shipped cross-country. So limit your searches to sources within driving distance, and never purchase a rabbit without first inspecting it in person!

❧❧❧

Searching for a new bunny companion can be exciting, as you meet lots of new bunny prospects and have a chance to talk to knowledgeable rabbit fanciers. It can be tempting to rush into rabbit ownership so you can get into rabbit-keeping as soon as possible, but take your time! Try to enjoy your rabbit-shopping adventure, and learn as much as you can along the way. You probably wouldn't buy the first car you saw on the lot, and it doesn't hurt to shop around when looking for a new bunny, either.

CHAPTER FOUR

The Best Possible Beginning

Getting a new pet is as exciting as going on a first date, with the same tinge of nervous uncertainty. It's a time of adjustment. It's not easy to fit a new pet into your schedule. It's not easy for your bunny to adjust to a new environment, either. In fact, getting a new pet can affect the dynamics of your entire household! Adults,

Your new friend will be eager to spend time with you. Watching your rabbit's behavior can help you interpret what your pet needs and wants.

children, and pets alike will all face changes.

PREPARING FOR YOUR RABBIT

Planning the best possible beginning for your new hopper can help you avoid conflicts and stress during this adjustment period. More than that, it can provide a fun prelude to your adventure in rabbit ownership. So enjoy preparing for your new pet!

THE CAGE: The first order of business is to purchase all the supplies you will need to care for your bunny. The cage or indoor hutch is obviously the most substantial item, as it will serve as your pet's home. It will also take up some room in your house, so deciding where to put it is an important consideration.

Your indoor bunny will prefer a place with moderate traffic, as he'll want to watch the goings-on in the house without being overwhelmed by noise and activity. The high-frequency emissions from TV sets and microwave ovens are especially bothersome to bunnies. A place away from the drafts of windows and doors will help keep him healthy. Of course, he'll enjoy a place where he feels safe from the harassment of other pets.

Your rabbit's cage should have a minimum of four square feet of floor space (larger for really big bunnies), and be at least 18 inches (46 cm) high. When it comes to cages, bigger is always better, but keep it reasonable—remember, you have to clean it! Rabbits have a heavy layer of fur on the bottom of their feet that can tolerate wire-bottomed cages, but there should still be areas with solid flooring to prevent their hocks from getting sore.

Other features you may want to watch for include metal guards around the cage sides to prevent your playful bunny from kicking litter material all over the room, and a side door to make it easy for your pet to enter and exit his own cage when you open the door. A cage with multiple levels can give your pet a little more vertical space, which is even more desirable if you plan to house more than one rabbit in the same cage.

OUTDOOR HUTCH: Rabbits are weather-tolerant creatures that can do quite well with outdoor accommodations, but you should be aware that outdoor rabbits are more susceptible to illness, parasites, and predators. The hardships of being exposed to subzero winters, hot summers, humidity, and dampness will certainly shorten your pet's life span. Such a living arrangement will also make it difficult for you to bond very

You need to decide how close you want to be to your rabbits when considering whether to have them live inside the home or outside in a hutch. An outdoor hutch makes more sense when breeding rabbits, because of the space requirements.

closely with your rabbit. So if you want to keep a rabbit as a pet, keep it indoors where you can really enjoy each other's company.

If you plan to breed rabbits, however, it might be impractical to house them all in your home. There are a variety of outdoor hutches that are designed to house a number of breeding rabbits. Most of these have wire-mesh flooring that allow waste pellets to drop through to a collection tray for easy cleaning, but they should also have nest boxes and platforms for solid flooring.

Research your options thoroughly before purchasing an outdoor hutch, as some provide easier access to the inside of the cages and nest boxes. If you are ambitious enough to build your own hutch, you'll need 16-gauge wire mesh to prevent your little chomper from chewing his way out! Wood-frame hutches should be checked frequently for chewing damage and repaired as needed.

Just like indoor cages, outdoor hutches should be as large as possible, with a minimum of four square feet of floor space for a single rabbit. Does with litters need twice that amount of space. And all rabbits need a location out of direct sunlight and wind. A well-ventilated, airy garage can be a safe location for an outdoor hutch—but not if the garage is also used for cars, since exhaust fumes are toxic for rabbits.

For sanitary reasons, outdoor hutches should be raised off the ground by being placed on posts. Otherwise, they will attract vermin that like to burrow under them—a very unsanitary situation. Keep ease of cleaning in mind when you determine how high to set your hutches!

NEST BOX: Whether your bunny has a home indoors or out, he needs a nest box for his comfort and security. The nest box serves as a substitute "burrow" for domestic rabbits, and each rabbit deserves his own private nest box "space." It gives your rabbit a place to hide, rest, and keep warm. For outdoor bunnies, the nest box needs to be weatherproof and padded with plenty of hay for insulation. A burlap or felt flap over the doorway can help keep bitter winds out.

The nest box should be large enough for your rabbit to move around in it, but small enough to make him feel cozy. Since most nest boxes are constructed of wood, they need to be checked occasionally for gnawing damage. Repair or replace your bunny's nest box when necessary.

BEDDING: There are several reasons to put some type of bedding in your rabbit's cage. It helps absorb your pet's urine, making cage cleaning easier. It provides a soft footing that won't injure your pet's feet. And it serves as insulation, which can help keep your bunny warm.

A Flemish giant rabbit peeks his head out of his wooden nest box.

There are a number of good bedding choices, including ground corncob, wood shavings, hay, straw, and shredded paper. You might want to experiment with different types to see which one suits you the best. Cedar shavings should be avoided, however, as they are toxic to rabbits. Your pet will be safest if you stick to commercially packaged bedding, specifically designed for rabbits.

One of the greatest challenges in rabbit-keeping is minimizing urine odor, which can only be accomplished by cleaning your pet's cage frequently (every two to three days). To make this chore easier, you can line your rabbit's cage with newspaper before applying the bedding. This will help absorb any excess urine, and then you can simply roll the soiled bedding up in the newspaper when cleaning your pet's cage. You can also investigate products that chemically neutralize the ammonia in urine; these can be applied under the bedding. Don't use fragrances to cover up odors, as they can upset your bunny's delicate senses.

FEEDING SUPPLIES: Your pet's penchant for gnawing dictates that his feeding bowl should be made of a gnawproof material, such as ceramic or metal. Some rabbits think food dishes are toys and delight in tipping them over or flipping them around the cage. If this sounds like your rambunctious bunny, you may need to purchase a food dish that attaches to the side of his cage.

Rabbits can also make quite a mess of a water dish, which is why water bottles are the dispensers of choice for most rabbit owners. This can be attached to the outside of your pet's cage so he can't mess with it. A 16 ounce (454 g) bottle is large

RABBIT SUPPLY CHECKLIST

Cage or hutch
Bedding
Nest box
Chew toys
Food dish

Water bottle
Commercial feed pellets
Hay
Fresh greens or
  vegetables

Toenail clipper
Brush or comb
Pet carrier
Litter box

A water bottle mounted on the side of your rabbit's cage is a better option than a water dish, which your rabbit is likely to knock over.

enough for most rabbits. Even though rabbits aren't always heavy drinkers (depending on how much fresh food they eat) and the water supply may last for several days, their water should still be replaced with fresh water daily.

OTHER SUPPLIES: Other items you'll need to put on your shopping list include a brush or comb, a nail clipper, and a pet carrier. Even though your bunny does a pretty good job of grooming himself, a flea comb or small slicker brush can help keep your pet tidy during

molting season. A small pet nail clipper is just the right size to keep your bunny manicured and prevent problems with overgrown nails. And a small or medium-size pet carrier is a convenient place to keep your bunny when you're cleaning his cage. It's also an absolute necessity for transporting your pet to the vet, shows, or other places.

If you plan to litter train your pet, you'll need a small litter box that can fit in your pet's cage without taking up too much room. You can find litter boxes made specifically for small animals that have an opening in the side that make it easy for your rabbit to enter and exit the box.

Of course, you'll also need to find some toys for your pet. Even if these items are last on your list, they are not optional or low in priority. Toys and chewing objects are absolutely essential for your rabbit's physical and mental health! So have

FAST FACT

Rabbits are meticulous groomers that can get hairballs in their stomachs, just like cats. Brushing, especially during shedding season, can help prevent this problem.

some fun choosing cute, funny, and entertaining toys for your pet. Just make sure they are designed to be rabbit-safe.

BRINGING YOUR RABBIT HOME

All these preparations will ultimately lead to the happy outcome you've been looking forward to—bringing your rabbit home! You've done everything you can to make sure that your new bunny is comfortable. He has food and water, clean bedding, a secure hutch, a quiet nest box, and plenty of toys. What more could any bunny ask for?

Actually, there are two more things your rabbit needs to help him adjust to his new home: peace and quiet. It's natural to want to play with your new pet (some handling is fine), but try to give your new pet lots of time alone to become familiar and grow comfortable with his new surroundings. Too much excitement will just add to your bunny's stress level.

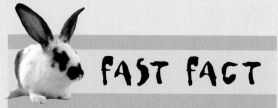

FAST FACT

An excited rabbit will pop into the air in a jump called a "binky." This is just one of the many ways a bunny expresses happiness.

One of the best ways you can develop a good relationship with your rabbit from the very beginning is to offer him treats of fresh food, like carrots or broccoli. Try to get your bunny to take the food directly from your hand. Your bunny will quickly learn what a great human being you are. He'll begin to trust you and may even begin to show his excitement whenever you approach his cage.

HANDLING YOUR RABBIT

Rabbits have amazingly powerful hind legs that can cause injuries to their owners and even themselves if they are not handled correctly. Aside from the scratches and bruises a bunny is capable of inflicting on humans, rabbits have been known to break their own backs if they kick violently enough.

The reason rabbits struggle is because they are uncomfortable about being lifted into the air. Their survival instincts make them feel much more secure on the ground, where they can flee to safety. Nevertheless, it's a good idea to teach your rabbit to tolerate handling by holding him frequently and gaining his trust.

Always use two hands to pick up and hold your rabbit. Scoop one hand under your rabbit's chest, and

To avoid injury, show members of your family the proper method of holding your rabbit. This young girl is holding the rabbit close to her, but should have one hand supporting his backside.

adults, it is best if they do not pick up rabbits. Children can have just as much fun, and your bunny will be much happier, if they play on the floor together. Some rabbits enjoy sitting on a lap to be petted, but most of them don't appreciate being carried around like a stuffed animal.

For rabbits that resist being handled, clicker training often helps overcome this troublesome behavior (see Chapter 7).

ESTABLISHING RULES AND RESPONSIBILITIES

The type of handling children will be allowed to engage in is just one of the rules you will need to establish. When, where, and how long children can play with the rabbit should also be made clear from the start. A rabbit that becomes stressed from too much or improper handling can resort to biting or other undesirable behaviors. So keep your bunny from

use your other hand to support his backside. Bring him immediately to your body so he doesn't feel like he's dangling in the air. You can hold him with his underside against your chest, or hold him securely in your arms against your stomach.

Since children do not have the same coordination and reflexes as

FAST FACT

Some rabbits, depending on breed, can jump up to 36 inches (91 cm) high! These athletic animals need opportunities to stretch those long legs and get some exercise.

becoming exhausted or irritable by controlling, limiting, and supervising playtime.

A child can develop a wonderful relationship with a rabbit when she is taught to respect the animal. Recognizing and respecting what the rabbit likes and dislikes can help build understanding and trust. Another way to teach a child to respect an animal is to include her in the animal's care. Assigning rabbit-care duties, like cage cleaning, feeding, and watering, does even more than teach a child responsibility and respect.

An animal bonds to the person who cares for him. So a child who has the opportunity to care for an animal also has the opportunity to experience a special human-animal bond.

INTRODUCING OTHER PETS

Other pets also need to respect the lagomorph member of your family. Dogs and cats should not be allowed to terrorize your bunny; such tension in the household can cause enormous stress for all the inhabitants of your home. The best way to introduce your new rabbit is to do it slowly.

Keep your pets separated by doors, gates, or other types of barriers so they can first become accustomed to each other from a distance. When they do not seem too concerned about each other's pres-

All of your household pets have the potential to be friends. It just may take a little time for them to adjust to one another.

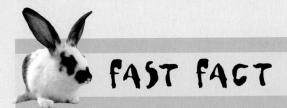

FAST FACT

Remember to give your other pets plenty of attention after bunny comes home, to avoid problems with jealousy.

ence, you can allow them to come closer to each other, but keep your bunny safely in his cage and observe your pets' interactions carefully.

If all seems to be going well, you can eventually allow your pets to sniff each other or meet each other on the floor. Even though dogs are a rabbit's natural enemy, some dogs and rabbits hit it off like long-lost relatives. You might even discover that your particular rabbit has become the "bunny boss" of the house! But if your dog has an exceptionally strong prey drive and can't control his urge to pursue your bunny, they will have to be kept separated.

ᘓᕝᘓᕝ

Preparing for your new pet is all about ensuring harmony. You can avoid conflicts, unpleasant surprises, and heartaches by thinking ahead. A well-planned beginning leads to a smoother transition, and this means you can focus on the thrill of your bunny's arrival. It is the first of many cherished memories you will create with your precious long-eared friend!

CHAPTER FIVE

Nutrition, Exercise, Grooming, and Training

In the wild, rabbits have a huge selection of plant material available to them to meet all their nutritional requirements. They receive plenty of exercise foraging for food, digging dens, and escaping from predators. They can take care of their own grooming needs and they don't have to be trained to be good house pets. Not so for your domestic rabbit!

Your rabbit will always respond to food. Use carrots and other treats to help with training.

Your bunny has the same needs as his wild ancestors, but he lives in an artificial, human-made environment. It is up to you to provide the variety of foods necessary to meet his nutritional requirements. The amount of exercise your pet gets depends entirely on how much time you let him play outside his cage and what activities you give him to do. You'll have to take care of some of his grooming needs, like trimming his nails, because he doesn't have the opportunity to wear his nails down naturally. You'll also have to teach your bunny to behave while being handled, because it's difficult to care for a bunny that you can't touch.

Caring for your rabbit does take some effort, but it also helps you develop a relationship with your pet. When you feed your bunny, he learns to look forward to seeing you. When you play with your bunny, he learns to enjoy your company. When you groom or handle your bunny, he learns to trust you. So allow these care duties to be what they really are—part of the fun of rabbit ownership.

NUTRITION

Rabbits don't just eat to live; they live to eat. Nature has programmed these voracious eaters to nibble constantly, but the wrong balance of food can cause diarrhea, constipation, or dietary deficiencies. In order to provide complete nutrition for your rabbit, make sure his diet contains three components: commercial rabbit pellets, fresh vegetation, and hay.

COMMERCIAL FEED: Commercially prepared rabbit pellets make bunny nutrition easy. They already contain all the vitamins, minerals, and important nutrients your rabbit needs for a balanced diet. So why not feed your

fEEDING TIPS: DO'S AND DON'TS

Do provide fresh food and water daily.

Don't feed your rabbit old, withered, or moldy foods.

Do feed your rabbit on a regular schedule.

Don't feed your rabbit any plant material unless you know for sure that it's safe.

Do measure your rabbit's food and monitor his weight.

rabbit nothing but commercial feed? Commercial feed is absolutely essential for your rabbit's health, but there are two problems with it: It's dry and it's rich.

Keeping your rabbit on a purely dry diet is sure to cause constipation, so the addition of moisture-laden fresh food is a must. Besides, there's nothing your bunny loves more than fresh greens, vegetables, and fruits—food in a form that nature intended! Remember how your bunny loves to nibble? Too much nibbling on nutrient-rich rabbit feed can turn your healthy hopper into a bulging bunny, so limit your pet's consumption of pellets, and supplement his diet with good-quality (but lower-calorie) hay to satisfy his urge to chew.

FRESH VEGETATION: Fresh vegetation to rabbits is like apple pie to

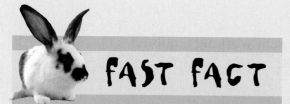

FAST FACT

Whether the fresh food you supply is from your yard, your garden, or the grocery store, it is always a good idea to remove any residual pesticides, herbicides, or fertilizers by washing it before giving it to your pet.

FAST FACT

How much water your rabbit drinks depends on how much moisture he is receiving from his fresh foods. Even when it seems as if your pet is drinking almost nothing, you still need to replace his water with fresh water daily.

humans. Rabbits love their fresh foods, and your bunny will be sure to let you know which ones he likes the best. Providing fresh foods for your rabbit can be as easy as saving the vegetable, fruit, or salad shavings from your kitchen, or picking grass outside your front door. Rabbits adore carrots, broccoli, asparagus, spinach, apples, pears, dandelions, clover, and many other kinds of fresh foods.

There are only three rules that apply to fresh foods: They must really be fresh, they must be nontoxic, and their consumption should be limited. Your rabbit is not a garbage disposal for old, moldy, or withered produce. If you wouldn't eat it, your pet shouldn't, either. Stay away from any type of vegetation that may have been sprayed with chemicals, and be sure to wash any fresh foods you purchase from the grocery store before serving them to your bunny.

PLANTS THAT ARE TOXIC FOR RABBITS

Rabbits may love green foods, but that doesn't mean all green foods are safe for them. The following common plants are poisonous to rabbits:

Aloe vera	Gladiolus	Peony
Azalea	Holly	Philodendron
Begonia	Hyacinth	Poinsettia
Carnation	Hydrangea	Rhododendron
Chrysanthemum	Impatiens	Rhubarb
Clematis	Iris	Sago palm
Cone flower	Ivy	Tulips
Daffodil	Juniper	Wisteria
Daisy	Lilies	Yew
Eucalyptus	Mistletoe	
Geranium	Oleander	

(For a comprehensive list of plants that are toxic to rabbits, see the Sacramento House Rabbit Society Web page, www.allearssac.org/poison.html.)

Not all plants are safe for rabbits to eat, so if you're not sure, don't feed it to your rabbit. Fresh-picked grass and other plants tend to decompose rapidly and can also become toxic, so don't give your pet more than he will eat at one time. Be sure to always remove uneaten fresh foods from your pet's cage.

Just like commercial feed, too much fresh food isn't good for your bunny. It can give him diarrhea or upset the balance of his diet. A small amount provided daily is greatly appreciated by your rabbit and excellent for his health.

HAY: Hay doesn't contain nearly the amount of nutrients that are found in commercial feed or fresh vegetation, but it still serves a very important dietary function. Hay is roughage that keeps your rabbit's digestive system working smoothly and efficiently. In particular, it helps your bunny pass the hair he ingests during self-grooming and prevents obstructions caused by hairballs. A handful of hay a day keeps the veterinarian away!

Your rabbit will enjoy any type of good-quality grass hay, including timothy or oat hay, but he may show a preference for the sweeter flavor of

This rabbit munches on some Timothy hay, which is not only good for him, but delicious, too!

dust-free. If you slap the bale and a cloud of dust billows out of it, it's not fit for your rabbit's consumption.

Keep your hay in a dry place and cover the top of it to keep it from getting dusty. The sides should be left open to allow the hay to "breathe." If stored properly, hay will retain its nutritive qualities for over a year.

CECOTROPES AND COPROPHAGY

Rabbits have a rather odd eating habit that might strike you as being repulsive, but it is nature's way of providing certain nutrients that your rabbit cannot obtain in any other way. Rabbits produce cecotropes, which are softer waste pellets that are meant to be reconsumed. In fact, your rabbit will probably reingest these pellets directly from his anus without your noticing it.

If you do see your rabbit engaging in coprophagy, which is the term

an alfalfa mix. Pure alfalfa is much too rich, but a good mix, with up to 10 percent alfalfa, can please your pet's palate without making him put on the pounds.

Some pet supply stores sell hay, but you might get a better deal by asking a local farmer if he can spare a bale or two. This should be enough to last you most of the year if you are using it only for feed and not for bedding. Fresh hay is a light green color, not yellow or light brown. It should be mold-free and

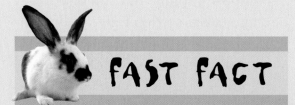

FAST FACT

If your rabbit seems to be getting more "plush" in appearance and his body feels soft and squishy, it may be time to put your pudgy bunny on a diet. Cut back on commercial rabbit feed and increase his intake of roughage (hay).

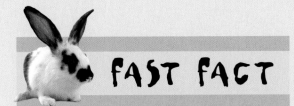

used when an animal consumes its own waste, don't be alarmed. There is nothing wrong with your bunny. This behavior is perfectly normal and necessary for your rabbit's health.

EXERCISE

In addition to a proper diet, your rabbit needs adequate exercise. He doesn't have to train for the Boston Marathon or a Mr. Universe title, but let's face it: A cage or hutch doesn't provide enough room for even a minimal workout. That's why your rabbit needs plenty of playtime outside his cage. Allowing your bunny to romp in a safe indoor or outdoor play area is both physically and mentally stimulating for your pet. (See Chapter 7 for instructions on creating a safe play area.)

You can encourage your pet to get the most benefit from his playtimes by providing toys and obstacles for him to explore, play with, and move around. Paper grocery bags make nice "dens" to crawl into. Cardboard tubes are fun for him to push with his nose and chew on. Spreading treats around the area will encourage your bunny to move around in search of them. Of course, having someone (like yourself or another pet) to play with makes playtime even more fun!

LITTER BOX TRAINING

How much time you are willing to allow your rabbit to spend outside his cage may depend on his house manners. Some rabbits require stricter supervision because of their destructive tendencies. Some rabbits are a little too curious for their own good and tend to get into trouble. You can't change your bunny's personality, but you can teach your rabbit at least one house manner that makes it easier to give him some household freedom: how to use the litter box.

Rabbits have a natural preference to eliminate in designated areas, perhaps related to an ancestral instinct

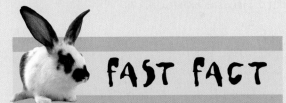

to avoid defecating in their dens. So the trick to litter box training your rabbit lies in convincing him that a litter box is a great "designated area."

You'll need to provide a litter box for your pet at all times, even when he's in his cage, because in order for him to develop a good habit, he needs to be able to do it frequently. Purchase a litter box designed for small animals and put it in your pet's cage where he has already established a potty area. Fill the bottom of the box with an inch (2.5 cm) of litter.

The best litter to use is an organic brand made especially for rabbits. These can be found where rabbit supplies are sold. Do not use clumping cat litter, as this can cause digestive obstructions if they are consumed by your pet. You'll need to place a few of your bunny's waste pellets in the litter to help your rabbit get the right

Litterbox training your rabbit can be challenging at first, but once he understands the concept, he'll get the knack quickly.

idea. Sometimes, putting some hay in the box will encourage your bunny to spend more time in it.

Don't be surprised if your rabbit decides he likes the box so much that he uses it for lounging! It's OK if he wants to use it for playing and sleeping, too, but if he starts targeting a different area of his cage for doing his business, move the litter box there and put plenty of his waste in it. Eventually, when he starts using the litter box regularly, you can start placing it on the floor when he is playing outside his cage.

Rabbits are not cats, and realistic expectations are in order. You can't expect your rabbit to use the litter box 100 percent of the time, although some rabbits become quite reliable at it. It helps to restrict your rabbit's play area during the training process; provide several litter boxes as well, so your pet doesn't have to travel very far to use one. Clicker training methods can also help in your endeavors to litter box train your rabbit (see Chapter 7).

GROOMING

Rabbits are almost obsessive about washing and grooming themselves, which means they are extremely clean animals. Aside from the long-haired varieties, most rabbits need little help from their humans to keep clean. If a rabbit appears to be dirty, it is because he is sick or his cage needs to be cleaned more often.

Still, all rabbits benefit from some grooming assistance. Brushing can reduce the amount of hair in your home and help teach your bunny to tolerate handling. Nails need to be clipped and teeth should be checked regularly to keep your bunny healthy. Best of all, grooming can be a pleasurable bonding activity.

BRUSHING AND COMBING: Brushing is seldom necessary for your self-grooming critter, but you might just discover that your bunny loves to be stroked with a soft-bristle brush or a rubber grooming mitt. Slicker brushes made for cats work well, as the thin metal tines have blunted tips to prevent you from

FAST FACT

When grooming or checking your rabbit's teeth, hold your pet's head gently. Do not steady him by holding him around the neck—you may accidentally cut off the blood supply through the jugular vein. This vein is close to the skin surface, rather than inside the neck as it is in other mammals.

scratching your pet's skin. Rabbits have relatively thin skin that can be injured easily by aggressive brushing or hair pulling. So be gentle!

Rabbits go through molting periods twice a year, in the spring and fall, when they shed their entire coat to make room for new hair growth. Rabbits kept indoors may molt more frequently. Removing the dead hair with a flea comb will help keep your pet neater and your house cleaner. It will also help prevent your bunny from getting bothersome hairballs.

Unlike the carefree coats of most rabbits, the angora breeds do require daily brushing. They are also more prone to mats, which need to be worked out carefully. Mats should be alternately pulled apart with fingers and brushed with a cat slicker brush. The hair should be held close to the

skin with one hand and brushed with the other hand to avoid pulling on the rabbit's delicate skin.

Regardless of your rabbit's hair type, grooming provides a good opportunity to check the condition of your rabbit's skin and coat. Backstroke your pet's fur so you can see the hair shafts and skin. If your rabbit has flaky skin, bald spots, or visible parasites, you should consult your veterinarian for treatment.

HAIR TRIMMING: Trimming applies solely to the angora breeds, and it should only be done during the warmer seasons for outdoor rabbits. Trimming during cold seasons can actually cause your pet to suffer hypothermia. If the idea of trimming your rabbit makes you nervous, you should consider a different breed of rabbit. Long-haired rabbits are only for those who are willing to groom and trim their high-maintenance coats!

You can trim your pet's coat with scissors to whatever length you wish, but pay particular attention to your pet's rear end and underside,

Grooming your rabbit during his molting period will help him shed excess hair.

which are more prone to get soiled and matted. Extra care should be taken when trimming around the feet and head. For safety reasons, you should teach your rabbit to sit calmly for grooming. Get your bunny accustomed to sitting on a grooming board (available at pet stores or online) or in your lap for trimming.

Angoras can also be shorn with electric clippers. It's not nearly as difficult to learn how to use them as it seems. You should start out with clipper blades that leave the hair about one inch (2.5 cm) long, and practice first on your rabbit's body and sides. Use scissors to trim everything else. You can then progress to clipping more parts of the body and giving shorter cuts as you gain skill and confidence with the clippers. Sensitive areas, like the stomach of does (watch for the teats), the genital areas, and the legs and feet are best off being trimmed with scissors.

BATHING: Bathing is not recommended for rabbits, as it can be overwhelmingly stressful to them. In addition, it takes a rabbit's coat a long time to dry, which can make the animal subject to illness. Thanks to the rabbit's habit of fastidious grooming, bathing should not be necessary. However, the occasional hutch stains or other soiling can be removed with "spot cleaning."

Plain water or unscented baby wipes can be used to work out stains. For more stubborn marks, you can try 3 percent hydrogen peroxide. After cleaning, dry the area as thoroughly as possible with a towel. Then, put your bunny in a play area so he can move around and finish drying. In some cases—especially if your rabbit has a somewhat laid-back personality—a low-speed, low-heat

Though your bunny won't enjoy a bath in the traditional sense, when he gets dirty, cleaning him with a washcloth will do the trick.

hair dryer may help hasten the drying process.

SHOW GROOMING: Except for the angoras, most rabbits don't require intensive grooming to be shown. The ARBA show rules specifically forbid the use of powders, dyes, and other "grooming preparations" designed to alter the appearance or condition of a rabbit's coat. You won't find all the deceptive grooming practices employed at dog or horse shows at an ARBA show, but that doesn't mean there are no tricks of the rabbit-grooming trade.

Use pet clippers to keep your domestic rabbit's nails trimmed to the right length.

Rinseless rabbit shampoos, which are available through select pet catalogs, are often used to bathe show rabbits without stressing them out. Wiping a rabbit with a damp cloth is the perfect way to remove loose surface hair from a show rabbit's coat. Gently rubbing a rabbit's fur with an anti-static spray designed for pets can make his coat more manageable. All these things are learned by observing and consulting with experienced showgoers. If you want to learn the best way to groom your particular breed of rabbit, talk to your breeder, attend shows, join a breed club, and befriend other rabbit fanciers.

NAIL TRIMMING: Part of every rabbit's grooming regimen should include nail trimming. Rabbits' nails grow continuously to compensate for wear, but, unfortunately, domestic rabbits do not do enough digging and running to keep their nails worn down. Long nails can cause injuries to both rabbits and their handlers.

You may need to trim your rabbit's nails every six to eight weeks, depending on how fast they grow. To do this, you'll need a small pet nail clipper, like that used for cats or small dogs (or a human nail clipper for a dwarf-size rabbit). Clip off just the pointy tip of your pet's nails. If you cut them too short, you may cut into the quick (the nail's blood supply), which can cause pain and bleeding. If your rabbit has white nails, the quick should be visible as a dark center within the nail. If your rabbit has dark-colored nails and you cannot see the quick, it is always best to leave the nails a little long, rather than cutting them too short.

If you do cut the quick, the nail will bleed for a short time. If you have a styptic pencil, you can dab it on the end of the nail to help stop the bleeding. Corn starch will also help clot the blood and stop the nail from bleeding.

Rabbits are not particularly fond of having their feet handled, but they do get used to it when you do it frequently. So handle your pet's feet often, even when you don't intend to trim his nails. Your bunny will probably be most comfortable, and you'll have better control over him, if you hold him in your lap for his pedicure. Most rabbits behave quite well when they have learned to trust their owners, but if you have a particularly high-spirited bunny, you can try to hypnotize him to make nail clipping easier (see Chapter 7 to learn how to do this)! After you're finished trimming your rabbit's nails, it's a good idea to give him a treat. This will teach your rabbit that he'll be rewarded each time his nails are trimmed.

HEALTH CHECK: Grooming isn't just a way to make your bunny beautiful; it also gives you a chance to assess your pet's health. It's easy to detect lumps, bumps, scrapes, cuts, and bald spots when you are already going over your rabbit's body with a brush. It's only natural to notice any problems with your pet's legs and feet while you're trimming his nails. While you're at it, you might also take a peek at your rabbit's nose, eyes, ears, and teeth.

Any sign of discharge, infection, itchiness, sensitivity, or misaligned teeth can indicate that your rabbit's health isn't at its peak. Depending on the symptoms, veterinary care may be warranted. Since the prognosis of many health problems depends on early detection, train yourself to be observant while grooming your little friend. It could very well mean the difference between a cure and a not-so-pleasant alternative.

❧❧❧

Even if he can't say it, your rabbit really does appreciate everything you do for him. He looks forward to the food and treats you bring him. It makes him feel good to have a clean cage. And having that molting hair combed out surely feels as good as a massage. No wonder bunnies are so affectionate toward their caregivers!

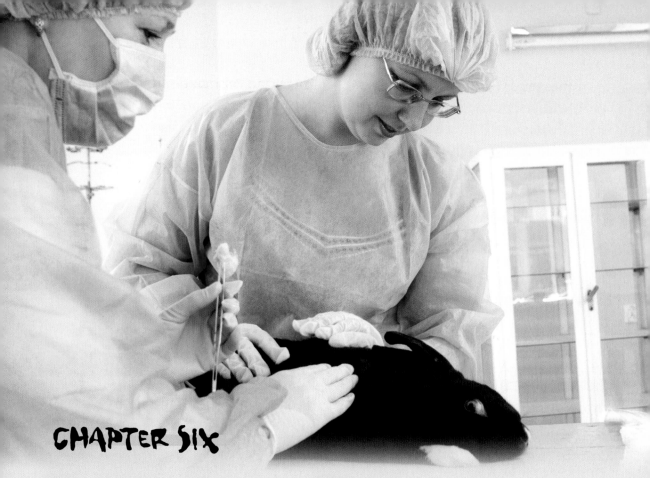

CHAPTER SIX

Health Issues Your Rabbit May Face

Your meek, mild-mannered rabbit is actually a member of a tough, adaptable species. Many rabbits go through life with nary a sick day, but those who do get sick are expert at concealing their symptoms. This behavior carries over from their wild ancestry. Predators view sick animals as easy meals so, in the interest of self-preservation, rabbits try to hide such weaknesses. Would you be able to recognize a rabbit's subtle signs of ill health?

Finding a veterinarian who is experienced at treating small mammals like rabbits is an important responsibility for new pet owners.

Illnesses are not the only health issues that may face your rabbit. As many rabbit owners have discovered, rabbits are as curious as cats. This puts them at risk of getting into dangerous situations, but unlike felines, they are not known to have nine lives! Their skittish, prey animal behavior also makes them prone to accidents. Would you know what to do if your rabbit got hurt?

CHOOSING A VETERINARIAN FOR YOUR RABBIT

You can't be expected to recognize the symptoms of every rabbit disease, but you can enlist the help of someone who can. The best thing you can do for your rabbit's health is to choose a veterinarian who is knowledgeable about rabbits.

While veterinarians are educated in the health needs of many kinds of animals, there are far too many different species of animals for a veterinarian to become an expert in all of them. That's why many veterinarians pursue specialties. Veterinarians who are interested in lagomorphs acquire additional education in so-called "exotics."

To find a qualified exotics veterinarian, you can ask a local rabbit club, breeder, 4-H club, or rabbit rescue group for recommendations. You can also check the member listing at the Association of Exotic Mammal Veterinarians (AEMV) Web site, www.aemv.org, to find an exotics vet in your area.

Locating a vet is only half the work, though. Once you have found a vet who is within reasonable distance of your home, you should evaluate the veterinarian to make sure she is a good match for you and your bunny. The best way to do this is to conduct an interview in person, which can often be done when you take your pet in for his initial exam.

You can expect an exotics vet to be knowledgeable about rabbits, but does she also indicate an in-depth knowledge of rabbit behavior? Is she compassionate toward your bunny, and does she explain things in layperson's terms to you? Most important,

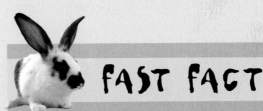

FAST FACT

Symptoms of illness do not always come in a physical form, such as nasal discharge or hair loss. Sometimes they are expressed behaviorally. Is your rabbit acting uncharacteristically aggressive? Is he overly lethargic? Or is he behaving strangely? Always be observant of your bunny's behavior.

does she appear to be someone whose judgment you can trust?

Graduating from veterinary school cum laude is admirable, but a veterinarian must also have an exemplary staff who supports her. Are the office personnel and veterinary technicians professional and competent? Are you and your pet treated with courtesy and respect? If you receive the best of treatment during a routine exam, you can expect excellent care in an emergency as well.

THE FIRST VETERINARY EXAM

A veterinary exam for any newly acquired rabbit is very important. If there are any pre-existing health conditions, it helps to detect these right away, especially if health guarantees apply. You want to make sure your new rabbit doesn't have any illnesses or parasites that might be passed on to other pets (or humans). This initial vet visit also gives you a chance to ask your vet any questions you may have concerning your new pet's health or behavior.

Your veterinarian should conduct a thorough exam, which includes checking your pet's heart, lungs, abdomen, skin, mouth, eyes, ears, and nose. If your new bunny has any pre-existing conditions, he will often show signs in one of these areas. After your rabbit receives a clean bill

of health, you can discuss the necessity of vaccinations and neutering for your pet.

VACCINATIONS

There are two rabbit diseases for which vaccines exist: myxomatosis and viral hemorrhagic disease. These vaccines are not approved for use in the United States, but they are commonly used in Europe, where these diseases are of greater concern. In the United States, management practices must be used to control outbreaks of any type of disease. This includes taking measures to prevent domestic rabbits from coming into contact with wild rabbit populations; preventing contact with other domestic animals, like dogs and cats; using screens or sprays to prevent contact with mosquitoes and

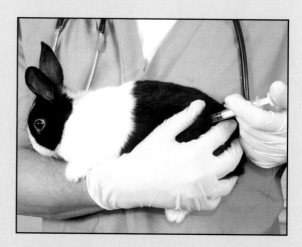

A simple vaccination can prevent two viral diseases that affect pet rabbits.

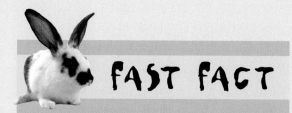

FAST FACT

It is a good practice to quarantine a new rabbit from other rabbits to make sure he does not have a contagious condition. A reasonable quarantine period is two weeks, during which time any existing disease should become apparent.

flies; and isolating or culling sick rabbits.

MYXOMATOSIS: Myxomatosis is a devastating viral disease spread among wild rabbits. It is also known as "mosquito disease" or "big head disease." This disease can also affect domestic rabbits, especially those kept in outdoor hutches. Its horrific symptoms include swelling of the eyes, ears, nose, and lips, and the eventual infection of the brain, which results in death. It is spread by insects, such as flies, mosquitoes and fleas, and there is no cure for it. Vaccination doesn't always prevent a rabbit from contracting this virus, but it greatly improves his chances of recovery.

VIRAL HEMORRHAGIC DISEASE: Viral hemorrhagic disease, referred to as VHD, can also be acquired from either wild rabbits or infected domestic rabbits. Symptoms include fever, lack of coordination, bloody nasal discharge, and pain. This incurable disease causes widespread hemorrhaging of internal organs, and usually results in death. Fortunately, it is not very common in the United States, as the wild rabbit species in this country are not susceptible to it.

NEUTERING AND SPAYING

There are two major reasons why your indoor rabbit should be neutered or spayed. For one, altered rabbits simply make better pets. Second, the huge population of homeless rabbits doesn't require your rabbit's assistance to grow larger.

In addition, intact rabbits are difficult pets to maintain. Bucks are almost impossible to litter train, as they are hormonally driven to spray urine throughout their environment. Worse than that, they can become quite dominant and aggressive, often

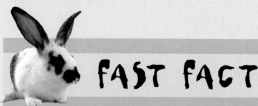

FAST FACT

Rabbits are not immune to hereditary health problems. Malocclusion, epilepsy, and spastic paraplegia (paralysis) are just a few of the hereditary disorders that affect rabbits.

chasing and attacking humans (or other pets) who are on the receiving end of their ire. The aggression of intact does can also present a problem, as does often become territorial and nippy. Nobody likes a rabbit that bites! So if you really want to see how sweet and gentle your bunny can be, have your pet neutered or spayed.

When it comes to rabbit overpopulation, neutering and spaying is simply the right thing to do. But there are other considerations as well. Intact does are at a very high risk of developing uterine cancer. If intact rabbits are denied the opportunity to mate, it can cause physical problems for them. Remember, nature has designed this species to procreate frequently and rapidly. If you are not serious about rabbit breeding, any rabbits you adopt will be much healthier if they are neutered or spayed.

PARASITES

One of the most important reasons for having your new bunny examined by a veterinarian is to make sure that your rabbit hasn't been keeping the worst kind of company: worms and bugs. These little critters may give you the creepy crawlies, but in most cases, they do little harm to your rabbit. When they overpopulate to the point of causing symptoms, your veterinarian can recommend treatment, but it is easier to avoid parasite problems by employing good husbandry practices—keeping cages clean and quarantining new rabbits.

MITES: Like most parasites that live on the surface of animals, mites can cause intense itching and discomfort for your rabbit. Some mites prefer the moist environment inside rabbits' ears and will cause red spots and patches of hair loss, referred to as "ear canker." Scratching can further damage the skin and leave the ears irritated and scabby.

Other mites target different parts of the body and cause bald or crusty

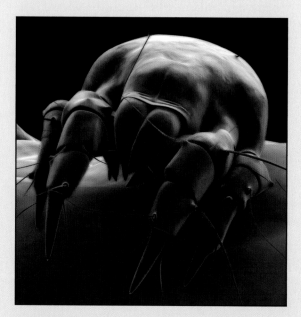

Fur mites like this can cause severe skin infections. Mites are worst in the springtime.

FAST FACT

Insects, such as mosquitoes, flies, fleas, and ticks, serve as carriers for disease. You can keep your rabbit from becoming ill by minimizing your pet's exposure to insects. House your rabbit indoors or use screens to protect him outdoors. Make sure your other household pets are pest-free. And treat pest infestations promptly and thoroughly.

patches, a condition called "mange." You can't see these tiny insects with your eyes, but your veterinarian can check for their presence by magnifying a scraping of your pet's skin. After proper diagnosis, your vet can prescribe the best course of treatment, depending on the severity of the condition. Mites can be passed on to other pets, so an infected rabbit should be quarantined until after the full course of treatment, which may include several applications of a topical medication.

WORMS: It's not unusual for plant eaters to ingest worm eggs and become infected with intestinal worms. Roundworms, tapeworms, and pinworms are occasionally found in rabbits, but treatment is rarely necessary unless symptoms of diarrhea, weight loss, or listlessness occur. If you notice some worms in your rabbit's feces, but your rabbit appears to be in overall good health, this is usually not a cause for concern.

Worms can be controlled by keeping cages clean and minimizing the chance that fecal pellets will contaminate food or water. Dogs are often the source of tapeworms, so it is important to make sure that any dogs that come in contact with your rabbit are parasite-free. If your rabbit is allowed to play outdoors, make sure he doesn't play in areas where dogs defecate.

FLEAS: Fleas are blood-sucking parasites that live on the skin surface. The most obvious sign of fleas is the animal's frantic scratching, which may eventually result in skin damage or hair loss. You can confirm the

Other pets in your home can transmit fleas to your bunny.

presence of fleas by backstroking your pet's hair to see tiny dark bugs scurrying along the skin.

Fleas come in a variety of species: Some prefer rabbits; some prefer other types of animals. However, they are opportunistic feeders, and if the right species of animal isn't available, they will target the next best thing. That means that a rabbit can become infested with rabbit fleas, dog fleas, or cat fleas. Getting rid of an infested rabbit will not necessarily get rid of the fleas; in fact, some fleas will begin to target humans if there are no animal hosts available.

You must eradicate these pests by treating your pet and his environment—that includes his cage, your home, and his outdoor play areas. To treat your rabbit, use a product recommended by your vet.

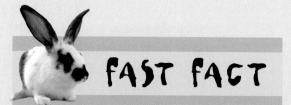

FAST FACT

One ounce (28 g) of bleach mixed with a quart (1 litre) of water is an effective and inexpensive disinfectant that can be used on cages, hutches, nest boxes, water bottles, and feeding equipment. Clean the items first, apply the solution with a spray bottle, and then let them dry before returning your pet to his cage.

Never use a flea dip or shampoo on your bunny! If you have other pets that also need to be treated, only use products formulated for the appropriate species, as insecticides made for one species are not necessarily safe for another species.

Insecticidal sprays or foggers can be used to treat your rabbit's environment, but it is a good idea to keep your rabbit out of treated areas until the effects have dissipated. You will have to treat your rabbit and his environment at least twice to completely resolve the problem.

COCCIDIOSIS: There are several species of microscopic parasites, called *coccidia*, that can invade a rabbit's intestines or liver, causing the disease *coccidiosis*. The intestinal species can be quite harmful, causing symptoms of diarrhea and weight loss that often result in death. Again, the control of this parasite involves meticulous management practices to minimize rabbits' exposure to infected feces. Infected rabbits should receive veterinary care as soon as possible to improve their prognosis.

COMMON HEALTH CONDITIONS

Parasites can make your rabbit miserable, but they are rarely life-threatening (with the exception of coccidia). Not so with some health conditions. Thanks to your rabbit's skill at concealing symptoms, many health conditions can reach a critical stage before you even notice that something is wrong. So be observant of your bunny's condition and behavior, and seek veterinary treatment as soon as you spot signs of illness.

RESPIRATORY INFECTIONS: Upper respiratory infections start out with coldlike symptoms, such as sneezing and nasal discharge, which can eventually progress to an infection in the lungs (pneumonia). Often called "snuffles," due to the sound an infected rabbit makes as it breathes, an upper respiratory infection may or may not respond to a broad-spectrum antibiotic. Infected rabbits should be segregated from other rabbits. Since the symptoms of respiratory illness are similar to those associated with

dental problems and other maladies, your veterinarian is the only one who can make an accurate diagnosis.

MALOCCLUSION: The rabbit's teeth are an efficient eating tool, designed to grow continuously in order to withstand the constant wear of grazing. Unfortunately, when a rabbit's teeth aren't aligned properly, they do not wear properly, and this malocclusion can cause significant problems. Teeth will become overgrown, resulting in mouth sores and difficulty eating.

Symptoms of malocclusion include drooling (a wet chin), lack of appetite, or discharge from the nose or eyes. There is no cure for this genetic problem, but it can be managed with regular tooth trimmings performed by your vet. Your veterinarian may even show you how to trim your pet's teeth yourself.

SYMPTOMS THAT WARRANT A VISIT TO THE VET

Refuses to eat	Tilted head	Moves reluctantly
Feces production has ceased	Loss of balance	Severe swelling
	Paralysis	Head shaking
Teeth grinding from pain	Blood in stool	Bald patches
Difficulty breathing	Constant trembling	Bloated belly

DIARRHEA: Diarrhea, which is the production of soft or runny stools, can be caused by illness or diet. An abrupt change in diet is often the culprit, with the consumption of too many fresh foods being the main contributing factor. Fresh vegetation must be balanced with dry foods to avoid just such a problem. As much as your bunny looks forward to fresh grass in the spring, limit his outdoor grazing time in the beginning of the season to give his system a chance to adjust to the abundance of greens. Cut back on greens and provide more hay if diarrhea develops. Also, make sure the fresh food your pet receives is not moldy or laden with chemicals.

If diet is ruled out as the cause, or there are other symptoms that accompany the diarrhea, see your veterinarian immediately. Diarrhea that persists for several days can be deadly for such a small creature.

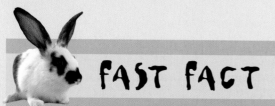

FAST FACT

Liquid medications can be administered to your rabbit with a syringe-type dispenser. Place the tip of the dispenser into the side of the mouth, behind the incisor teeth, and depress the plunger slowly.

CONSTIPATION: Constipation is another condition often related to your pet's diet. Like other grazing animals, the rabbit's body is designed to constantly process food. Horse owners assess the health of their "hay burners" by keeping a close eye on the waste they produce, and your rabbit can also benefit from this practice. If your bunny does not eliminate regularly, or his stools are smaller or harder than usual, he may be constipated. Cutting back on dry foods and increasing your rabbit's fresh rations should resolve the problem.

If diet does not appear to be the cause, or your rabbit appears to be straining or in pain when he's defecating, consult with your veterinarian immediately. A rabbit may get hairballs in his digestive tract, and these can cause potentially serious obstructions. A complete cessation of stool production requires emergency treatment.

You can prevent problems with hairballs by giving your rabbit access to an unlimited supply of hay. Regular exercise also helps to keep things "moving." There are laxative products for rabbits on the market— a regular dose once a week can be a good preventive for a bunny that tends to have problems with hairballs.

OBESITY: Rabbits are supposed to eat frequently. It keeps their digestive tract functioning and also helps to wear down their teeth. If a rabbit becomes obese, it is not because of how much he eats; it's because of what he eats. If your bunny is getting a little roly-poly, it's time to replace some of his rich feed with lower-calorie items.

Too many rabbit pellets, too much alfalfa in the hay, or too many sweet fruits are usually the cause of excess weight gain. You'll need to cut back on pellets and switch to a purely grass hay. Avoid feeding him fruits

and vegetables that are high in sugar and starches, and make sure your rabbit has plenty of opportunities for exercise. A great feeding practice is to measure pellets and fresh foods so you can keep track of your pet's consumption. Then you can adjust your pet's diet as needed.

BLOAT: Many health conditions can be avoided by feeding your rabbit a balanced diet and adhering to good feeding practices. Bloat is one such condition. It is often caused by putting a rabbit on grass too suddenly, as a large amount of grass in the digestive tract can ferment in the gut and create gas. The gas causes the rabbit's stomach to expand noticeably. Veterinary treatment for this condition is imperative, because bloat is potentially fatal. Again, avoid sudden diet changes and limit your pet's time on grass.

EYE INFECTIONS: Conjunctivitis is an eye infection often referred to as "weepy eye." It causes a copious discharge from one or both eyes that can literally seal the eyes shut. The bacteria that cause this problem tend to flourish when rabbits are kept in crowded conditions. Cleaning the affected eyes and treating them with an antibiotic ophthalmic ointment can remedy the

Don't let your bunny get too fat! Put him on a diet and let him run more if he starts to appear overweight.

problem. Proper sanitation and housing can help prevent recurrences.

EAR INFECTIONS: You can imagine that a rabbit with an ear infection feels as bad as a giraffe with a stiff neck. Inner ear infections in rabbits are often characterized by a loss of balance and a tilted head (a symptom often called "wry neck"). Many rabbits respond well to a course of antibiotics, prescribed by a veterinarian. Since ear infections can be caused by different types of bacteria, and the symptoms are similar to a mite infestation, your veterinarian will need to do a culture in order to determine the correct diagnosis and treatment.

FUNGAL INFECTIONS: Ringworm is a common fungal infection that can be spread among domestic animals and even humans. It is not caused by worms, but actually gets its name from the circle of skin that it affects. The result is a round, bald patch of scaly or crusty skin, which gradually grows in size. Since the symptoms are very similar to those caused by mites, only your veterinarian can make a correct diagnosis by examining a scraping of your rabbit's skin.

Fortunately, this condition is treatable with the proper fungicide prescribed by your vet. Because this fungus is easily transmitted to humans—especially children—everyone in your household should avoid handling your pet until the problem is resolved. Your infected rabbit should be isolated from other rabbits and other pets as well.

INJURIES

Accidents can't always be avoided. But there are certain preventable injuries to which rabbits are particularly prone. Abscesses, sore hocks, and broken backs are all too common among domestic rabbits, although they don't need to be.

ABSCESSES: The most common cause of abscesses in rabbits is bites from other rabbits. Those long incisor teeth can inflict deep puncture wounds, which set the stage for bacterial infections. Intact bucks are notorious for fighting, but even neutered and spayed rabbits will fight if personality conflicts erupt.

To avoid fights, keep incompatible rabbits separated. If you are looking for a rabbit companion for your pet bunny, conduct a compatibility test first.

If your rabbit develops an abscess, you'll need to drain the abscess frequently by squeezing it gently. Follow up by cleaning the area with antiseptic until it heals. For severe abscesses, seek veterinary assistance.

SORE HOCKS: Sore hocks are indicated by a loss of hair and the subsequent development of sores on a rabbit's hind legs. These injuries can be painful for a bunny. They are usually the result of irritation caused by wire-bottom cage floors. Your rabbit should have solid flooring in at least a portion of his cage or hutch to get some relief from the abrasive wire. Check your pet's hocks frequently for loss of hair—it is easier to correct this problem before the skin becomes damaged. A piece of rug or a carpet swatch on the cage floor can help the legs to heal. Heavier rabbits, or those with thinner hair on the legs, may be more susceptible to this problem.

BROKEN BACKS: Paralysis of the hind legs is usually an indication a rabbit has broken his back. A rabbit's hind legs are so powerful that a violent kick can potentially dislocate a vertebra in his back and damage the spinal cord. This can occur when a rabbit engages in "thumping" (stomping his rear feet as a form of defensive behavior or dominance communication) on flexible flooring, like a wire-bottom cage. It is also a tragic result when a rabbit kicks while being held without any support for his rear legs. Some rabbits, due to their genetics, are at greater risk for this injury than others.

In most cases, humane euthanasia is the kindest option for the animal, so it pays to take precautions to prevent broken backs. Always hold your pet properly with support for the hind legs, and encourage children to play with the rabbit on the floor, rather than holding him.

❧❧❧

Many illnesses that affect rabbits share the same symptoms, which can make it difficult to determine the cause of a health problem. But the most important thing is to be able to recognize when something is wrong. A rabbit's health can deteriorate very rapidly, so your diligent observations are the key to helping your bunny live a long and healthy life.

CHAPTER SEVEN

Enjoying Your Rabbit

Rabbits are sensitive, expressive, and fascinating creatures. You can get an awful lot of entertainment value out of your rabbit simply by observing him. But there are many other wonderful activities that can maximize your fun, while giving you the opportunity to develop a stronger, closer bond with your pet.

PLAYTIME

Your rabbit is naturally curious and playful, but playtime means more than just getting you and your pet to engage in amusing activities. Playing

Rabbits are relatively long-lived, so you should be able to enjoy your pet for many years.

keeps your bunny fit and smart. It's not just a matter of giving your rabbit a nice large area in which to stretch his legs, as some rabbits will sit in a corner and do nothing at all. Playing involves interactions, toys, stimulation, and exploring. When it comes to keeping your bunny busy, use your imagination!

INDOOR PLAY AREA: An indoor play area usually consists of a suitable room where your pet can play on the floor, but it can also be a child's playpen, a puppy pen, or any other large indoor enclosure. When choosing a room to use as your rabbit's playground, always put safety first. Doorways must have sufficient barriers to keep your rabbit in and other pets out, if necessary. Items like electrical cords and wood furniture may need to be removed or covered, depending on your pet's propensity to chew on them. Any small areas

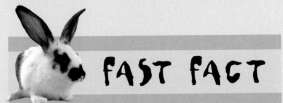

FAST FACT

It may seem desirable to put your bunny on an easy-to-clean vinyl floor to play, but smooth surfaces are slippery and can cause accidents. Put down some non-skid rugs to give your pet surer footing.

where your rabbit may become stuck, such as under couches or appliances, must be blocked off with cardboard or other materials.

You should supervise your rabbit closely, in case your furry friend discovers any hazards that escaped your attention. Then, depending on your rabbit's personality and his reliability when it comes to litter box training, you can consider gradually allowing your bunny more freedom in the house. Just be sure to take precautions so your little house-hopper doesn't manage to escape through an open door! And never allow your bunny to roam the house when you're not home—put him safely in his cage before you go out.

The easiest (and most fun) way to keep your bunny out of trouble when he is carpet cruising is to give him something interesting to do! Wood chew blocks, paper grocery bags, and cardboard tubes are all fun, safe toys for your pet. An obstacle course of pillows, blankets, chairs, and stools can mentally challenge your brainy bunny. A trail of small carrot chunks will keep your bunny on the "right path," or you can hide the treats in not-too-inconspicuous spots to keep your pet moving around as he hunts for them.

If you provide regular playtimes and make them fun for your pet, your rabbit will anticipate these activities with great enthusiasm! How many "binkies" (high jumps of happiness) can you get out of your bunny?

OUTDOOR PLAY AREA: Rabbits love playing outdoors, too, provided they can do so in a quiet area unmolested by dogs or other predators. The greatest attraction of spending time outside is access to that wonderfully fresh, sweet-tasting green stuff called grass! A portable 5-by-5-foot pen can be moved to different locations in the yard to provide a continuous source of this delectable treat. It can

Allowing your rabbit regular play time outside is good for him. Just make sure he's in a safe area, and watch to keep him out of trouble.

FAST FACT

Giving your rabbit too much room to play outside his cage can actually overwhelm him, so start out small. Give your rabbit a chance to become comfortable with a smaller space before offering him more room.

also be moved out of the way for easy lawn mowing.

As tempting as it may be to use a portable puppy pen for this purpose, your rabbit's outdoor play pen must have a top to prevent airborne predators from snatching your pet, and a bottom to prevent your pet from burrowing under the pen and escaping. A metal-mesh bottom of 14- or 16-gauge wire will allow grass to penetrate the bottom while keeping your bunny safe.

To avoid gastrointestinal problems, don't allow your bunny to eat a lot of fresh grass all at once, especially if he has been kept indoors for the winter. Gradually increase the amount of time your pet is on grass, and always provide a nest box haven in your bunny's outdoor pen to give him a place of shade and security.

You can also harness-train your bunny so you can take him outside on a leash. You can't expect your rabbit to walk on a leash like a dog, but you can offer your rabbit new territories to explore while keeping him safely within your reach. Always use a snug-fitting but comfortable harness, designed for a rabbit or other small pet, rather than a collar, as it is safer and more secure. To get your rabbit accustomed to wearing it, let him wear it frequently in the house at first. He will soon show no concern about donning it, and then you can take him safely outside to explore to his heart's content.

TRAINING

Your rabbit may not have the potential to become an Obedience champion, but that doesn't mean he can't be trained! Shaping behavior is something that can be done with all kinds of animals, including those as large as elephants or as small as mice. Training your rabbit is a matter of

FAST FACT

If you put your rabbit on a leash, use a soft, snugly fitting harness and allow your pet to wander in whatever direction his curiosity takes him. Rabbits cannot be trained to walk on a leash like a dog.

communicating to him what you want him to do, and then rewarding him for doing the right thing so he'll want to do it again. Imagine how impressed your friends will be when you show them that your rabbit is smart enough to come when called or fetches a toy for you!

CLICKER TRAINING: The easiest way to train a rabbit is through clicker training. This method of animal training involves using a clicker, which is a small, handheld device that makes a distinctive clicking sound. When your rabbit performs the correct behavior, you'll immediately give him a click, followed by a food reward, such as a piece of apple or carrot. It won't take long for your bunny genius to understand that when he hears a click, he gets a yummy treat! He'll then begin to figure out what he needs to do to earn clicks and treats.

When using a clicker to communicate with your rabbit, timing is crucial. If you click too soon or too late, you may end up confusing your bunny or, worse, teaching him the wrong thing. You need to click right at the moment your pet displays the correct behavior.

For instance, if you want to teach your bunny to come to the door of his cage when it's time to come out for playtime, give him a click when he moves toward the door. Don't wait until he has already been standing at the door for some time or he has started to walk away from the door.

Another good training tip is to teach your bunny in stages. When you first start teaching your bunny to come to his cage door, give him a click and a reward if he takes even one step in the right direction. Gradually expect him to take additional steps toward the door before clicking and rewarding him, until he eventually comes all the way to the door on his own.

Food rewards are a great way to encourage your bunny to repeat desired behaviors, but they can also function as "lures" to get your bunny to move the way you want him to. Wherever the food goes, your bunny will follow. Keep this in mind as you think of fun things to teach your bunny.

WHAT TO TEACH YOUR RABBIT: There are a number of useful and fun things you can teach your bunny. If you want your bunny to come when you call his name, lure him toward you with a treat while calling his name, then click and give him a treat. When your bunny seems to understand what he needs to do to

Food is a great motivator when training your rabbit. However, be careful not to overdo the snacks, or your pet will become overweight.

get the treat, you can increase the distance between you and your pet until your bright little bunny will come to you from across the room.

You can teach your bunny to go just about anywhere you want using this method. Lure your bunny to his cage, and then click and reward him. If you say "Home" to your bunny each time you do this, he will soon learn to go to his home on command. Think of the possibilities! You can teach your bunny to go through a "tunnel" or over a "bridge" on command. You can even teach your

bunny to do fancy maneuvers, like weaving between your legs, to entertain your houseguests!

Using food as a lure can help teach your bunny other kinds of tricks, too. Hold a treat above your bunny's head to lure him into a sit-up position, and then click and reward him. If you tell him to "beg" each time you do this, he'll soon be sitting pretty like a pro. You can find a wealth of clicker training tips and ideas in the book *Getting Started: Clicking with Your Rabbit*, by Joan Orr and Teresa Lewin.

The main thing to keep in mind about rabbit training is that you can't force a rabbit to obey you. You have to convince your bunny that he wants to do what you ask. In other words, don't expect your bunny to be blindly obedient. As long as you have reasonable expectations and keep it fun, you can have a great time challenging your bunny's intellect!

PROBLEM BEHAVIORS: Clicker training can also be used to solve problem behaviors. It should first be noted that many problem behaviors, including aggression and urine spraying, can be avoided or solved by neutering or spaying an indoor rabbit. Other behavior problems, like chewing, can be addressed by giving your bunny appropriate chewing materials, rearranging furniture, or bunny-proofing his play area. You can't blame a bunny for acting like a bunny!

It is very common for a bunny to become hard to handle when he learns that biting earns him freedom. It doesn't take long for a bunny to realize that if he bites when people try to hold him, he will be released. In order to retrain a bunny with this problem, you must not put your bunny down when he bites!

Wear heavy gloves for protection and pick your bunny up for only a second. Hold him securely against your body. If he doesn't bite, give him a click, release him, and reward him. If he tries to bite, keep holding him until he stops. When he stops, you can click, release him, and reward him. Practice this several times a day and gradually increase the time you expect your rabbit to

Wear heavy gloves to protect your hands from a biting bunny. Eventually, if he learns that biting is not effective, he will give up the practice.

tolerate being held. Your bunny will soon learn that biting rabbits do not get put down, but good little bunnies are rewarded.

HYPNOTIZING YOUR RABBIT

Did you know that rabbits can be put into a trancelike state? Hypnotizing your rabbit may be a fun experiment to try. Start by putting your rabbit on his back and support him in this position with a pillow on each side of him. Begin stroking his sides in the direction the hair lays and hum quietly to help your bunny relax. Then gently stroke his abdomen until he looks glassy-eyed.

Your bunny may remain in this position for several minutes, or until a noise or movement "snaps" him out of it! You'll have the best success if your rabbit is in a calm mood beforehand.

Hypnosis is also sometimes done to make nail clipping easier. (See Chapter 5.)

THERAPY PET

If you find that your particular rabbit has a strong affinity for humans and an amazingly docile temperament, you might feel guilty keeping such a special creature all to yourself. If you have a strong desire to share your pet with others, a therapy pet program can allow you to bring smiles to schoolchildren, nursing home residents, or others who need it.

Dogs are not the only animals that can provide companionship and unconditional love as therapy pets; rabbits can, too! But therapy work is not a job for an excessively skittish or high-strung rabbit. Therapy rabbits should be used to a lot of handling and able to deal with different environments. Former show bunnies may be good candidates, as are pet bunnies that receive and thrive on a lot of human attention.

There are a few things to keep in mind when employing a rabbit as a therapy pet. First, most rabbits are uncomfortable being held by strangers, and they have strong hind legs that can cause injuries if they try to escape. So it's best if you hold your own rabbit for others to pet. Some rabbits feel more comfortable on a solid, flat surface, so you may be able to present your pet on a piece of fabric-covered plywood that can be placed in people's laps. Some therapy rabbits are transported and presented (quite appropriately) in large Easter baskets!

Second, rabbits are small, delicate animals that do not particularly appreciate rough handling. Some children and elderly people do not always have the coordination and reflexes to safely handle a rabbit.

Rabbits make great therapy animals because of their cute appearance and gentle nature.

Since the safety of your pet is entirely in your hands, you must be willing to intervene quickly if you sense there may be a problem.

Third, the presence of dogs or other animal species may make your normally friendly and docile rabbit nervous. Be sure to schedule your therapy pet visits when other therapy animals are not already scheduled. This will help keep your little hopper from becoming "jumpy."

The Delta Society Web site, www.deltasociety.org, is a great place to find other valuable tips on therapy pet work. You might even consider having your bunny certified through its Pet Partners Program. You always have the option of "going it alone" and making your own visiting arrangements with various institutions, or you can network with a local pet therapy group. You can locate groups in your area by visiting the Therapy Dogs International Web site, www.tdi-dog.org.

SHOWING

A single win in the show ring is all it takes to get you hooked on the sport of rabbit showing! Awards and titles are just some of the benefits of taking your passion for rabbits to this level. You also get to travel, meet other rabbit fanciers, and show off your precious pride and joy! Can you think of a more fun way to spend your weekends?

There is one major consideration in deciding whether to get involved in the show circuit: Show bunnies cannot be neutered or spayed. The whole purpose of showing is to encourage the breeding of animals that possess exemplary characteristics. But breeding is not an endeavor to take lightly. Even though your rabbit is capable of reproducing easily and rapidly, it may not be an easy or rapid task to find homes for his progeny. Planning ahead is necessary if you want to avoid being inundated with bushels of bunnies!

Also, keep in mind that breeding is a way of managing rabbit stock. It is not a form of pet-keeping. Bucks that have not been neutered can become downright mean toward people or other animals. It's not uncommon for them to growl, bite, or even spray urine at their targets. Deciding to keep your rabbit intact is serious business, but if you are deeply passionate about becoming an avid rabbit fancier, the rewards of showing and breeding can more than adequately make up for the drawbacks.

ARBA Shows: If you want to turn your love for long-ears into a bona fide hobby, you need to get started in showing before you even acquire your first rabbit. First on the agenda is studying the standard for your chosen breed. This will be enormously helpful in choosing a show prospect worthy of the time and effort you will eventually put into it. The ARBA publishes breed standards for all the accepted rabbit breeds in its book, *Standard of Perfection*, which can be purchased directly from the ARBA Web site, www.arba.org.

Next, attend as many rabbit shows as possible. Not only will this help familiarize you with how these shows are run, but it will also put you in contact with many knowledgeable breeders. They can answer your questions, and one of them may become the source of your first show rabbit. You can check the appropriate ARBA district Web site to get a schedule of shows in your area.

When you have obtained a show rabbit, it will need to be registered with the ARBA. This is accomplished by becoming a member of the ARBA and having your rabbit examined by an ARBA registrar. Registration numbers are always tattooed on the underside of a show rabbit's left ear.

As a member of the ARBA, you will receive a newsletter that lists show locations and dates. It will be your responsibility to contact the secretary of each show you intend

to enter, so you can obtain entry forms and show information. Seeking the guidance of an experienced rabbit fancier can help you navigate this process the first few times. Show procedures will soon become second nature to you, and you'll be on your way to winning your first award! Some of the awards you might win include First in Class, Best of Breed, Best of Opposite Sex, and Best in Show. If you achieve enough of the right kinds of wins, your bunny may even become a Grand Champion!

4-H Shows: Children have their own venue for rabbit showing. The 4-H, which stands for "Head, Heart, Hands and Health," provides wonderful opportunities for young people to gain experience raising, caring for, handling, and showing animals. 4-H rabbit shows are conducted according to the same rules and breed standards as ARBA shows, with an emphasis on educating children in showmanship.

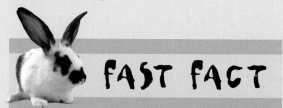

FAST FACT

The 4-H was started in the early 1900s as a way to connect public school education to country life.

A local 4-H club is a great place to start learning about rabbits and their care. This angora is on display at a 4-H show.

You can find links to district 4-H offices on the national 4-H headquarters Web site, www.national4-hheadquarters.gov. The district organization can then put you in touch with local clubs. The educational value of 4-H participation goes far beyond learning about rabbits. It offers valuable lessons that apply to many other animal species. It fosters the development of responsibility. And it provides a source of pride and success that only comes from hard work and diligence. This is one of the best ways for rabbits and children to come together.

BREEDING

Once your awesome bunny secures a few solid wins, you may be inspired to pass on his excellent qualities to subsequent generations of bunnies! The first requirement for a successful breeding program is adequate space. To maintain complete control over reproduction, you need to house bucks and does separately. You will also need double-size hutches to give your does enough room to raise their young.

INTRODUCING THE SEXES: Both bucks and does are sexually mature at around 6 months of age, but they should not be bred until they have reached physical maturity at 8 to 10 months of age. Does are receptive to breeding when they are in heat, and you can tell when your doe is ready by observing her behavior. She will seem restless and may begin to build a nest with hair plucked from her body.

When this happens, you can place the doe with the buck. Although rabbits do not need any instruction in the reproduction department, they do need to be supervised to make sure the mating goes well. If the female is not ready for mating, she

BREEDING TERMS

Crossbreeding: Mating two rabbits from different breeds.

Dewlap: A large fold of skin on a doe's neck, from which she plucks fur to line her nest. (In some breeds, males may have a small dewlap.)

Gestation: Length of pregnancy before birth. In rabbits this is about 31 days.

Inbreeding: Mating two rabbits that are closely related (e.g., sister to brother).

Junior: A rabbit less than 6 months old.

Kindling: Giving birth.

Kits or Kittens: Baby rabbits that are not yet weaned.

Line breeding: Mating two rabbits that are more distantly related (e.g., cousins).

Mastitis: Inflammation of the mammary glands (teats), often caused by removing the young from their mother too early.

Out-crossing: Mating two rabbits that are not related, but are members of the same breed.

Strain: Rabbits that are genetically related by bloodline.

Senior: Rabbits 6 months old and older.

may attack the buck, and you will have to separate the rabbits before injury occurs.

After mating, you can put the female in a double hutch so she can get on with the task of preparing a nest for her forthcoming brood. A nest box should be provided for her comfort, and her health should be monitored closely throughout her pregnancy. She will need constant attention in the later stages of pregnancy and during the birthing process; have your veterinarian's number handy. Quality feed—extra calcium and perhaps more commercial feed than usual—should be on the menu for pregnant and lactating does. Supplements generally aren't necessary unless the doe's condition warrants their use.

BABY BUNNIES: If all goes well, you'll be welcoming a bunch of baby bunnies 31 to 32 days after mating! Baby bunnies, which are called kits

or kittens, are extremely vulnerable, as they are born without fur and their eyes are sealed shut. It is important that you do not touch or disturb the newborn babies. Their eyes will open in 10 to 14 days.

The kits will begin to emerge from the nest at about three weeks of age, at which time they will also begin to consume some solid foods. Be sure to provide plenty of hay and a limited amount of greens. Weaning is a gradual process that allows the kits to develop the proper bacteria in their stomachs to handle solid foods, so they should not be removed from their mother too early. Kits are not fully weaned until they are at least eight weeks old.

Sexing very young bunnies is difficult, but it becomes easier as the kits become juveniles between two and four months old. The bunnies are approaching sexual maturity at this age and should be separated to prevent unwanted pregnancies. Hopefully, you have already arranged new homes for the rabbits you do not intend to keep, and have made accommodations for the rabbits you do intend to keep.

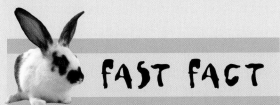

FAST FACT

Stress during pregnancy can cause a doe's fetuses to cease development. Instead of miscarrying, the fetuses are then reabsorbed by the doe's body.

TRAVELING WIITH YOUR RABBIT

Rabbit showing is just one of the reasons you may need to travel with your rabbit. There are also times

MALE OR FEMALE?

Determining the sex of adult rabbits is easy, as the scrotum of male rabbits is visibly prominent. It can be challenging, however, to determine the sex of young rabbits because of the immaturity of their genitalia. There are two openings under the rabbit's tail, the one closest to the tail being the anus and the other being the genitalia. If you place your index finger and middle finger on either side of the genitalia and apply gentle pressure to stretch the skin, you may expose the male penis or the female vulva.

when you may need to take your rabbit to a veterinarian, transport your rabbit for breeding purposes, or even move to a new home. In all these cases, there are some travel tips that can help make the journey more comfortable for both you and your pet.

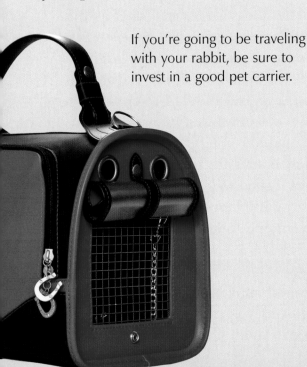

If you're going to be traveling with your rabbit, be sure to invest in a good pet carrier.

Your rabbit should be transported in a pet carrier for his safety. A plastic-sided carrier is a must, as your pet could injure himself in a wire cage. You can get your rabbit accustomed to this type of confinement by putting him in his carrier frequently before your trip. If you provide a favorite treat to keep him busy, he'll soon look forward to spending time in his big "nest box."

Then, when it's time to travel, your pet will be less stressed. If you plan on traveling a fairly long distance, you can further prepare your bunny by taking him for short drives around town so he can get used to the noises and vibration of vehicle travel.

It should go without saying that animals should never be left unattended in a closed vehicle, especially in hot weather. Leaving the windows cracked open will not be enough to

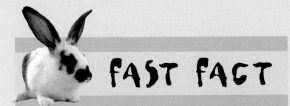

FAST FACT

When transporting your rabbit in a pet carrier, always secure the carrier with a seat belt.

keep the interior temperature of your vehicle from reaching a deadly level. If you must leave your pet in the vehicle for any reason, you should be prepared by purchasing a battery-operated car window fan ahead of time. You may also be able to leave your car running with the air conditioning on and the doors locked. If you need to stop for a meal along your route, opt for a fast food drive-through so you won't have to leave your pet unattended.

Traveling by plane is not recommended for rabbits. Airlines generally transport rabbits in a plane's cargo hold, where they are subjected to temperature extremes, a lack of pressurization, and a lot of noise. Such an environment is very taxing on a rabbit and could result in trauma, illness, or death.

PET SITTERS

Your rabbit isn't very interested in seeing new places; he much prefers a familiar, safe environment. So leave your pet at home when you take family trips, and don't transport him unless it is absolutely necessary. You

Check out www.petsitters.org to find a rabbit sitter in your area.

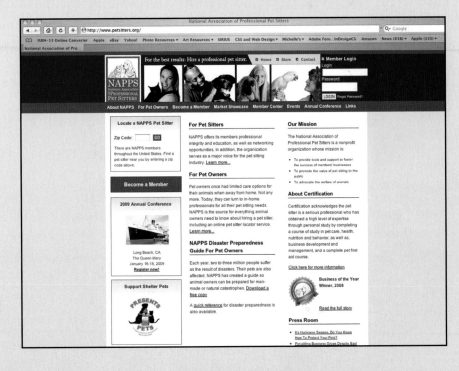

might be fortunate enough to have a friend, neighbor, or relative who is more than thrilled to care for your furry friend in your absence.

In that case, be sure to take the time to thoroughly instruct the person in rabbit care before you leave. It helps to show, rather than tell, the person what to do. Then, leave a checklist behind as a reminder. You should also include information on where you can be reached while you're gone, plus leave your veterinarian's phone number, in case of emergency.

If you have more than one pet, you might want to consider enlisting the help of a professional pet sitter. A professional pet sitter can take care of all your pets as well as watching over your home while you're

gone. You can find pet sitters through Pet Sitters International (www.petsit.com) and the National Association of Professional Pet Sitters (www.petsitter.org), both of which provide member listings on their Web sites.

When choosing a professional pet sitter, make sure the person lives up to the "professional" part of her job title. Conduct an initial interview with a prospective pet sitter, so she can meet you and your pets and get all the pertinent information about caring for your animals. A service contract she provides should spell out all the duties, guarantees, and fees of service. She should appear to be knowledgeable about and compassionate toward animals, and you should feel confi-

CHECKLIST FOR A PET SITTER

Don't forget to provide the following information for your pet sitter:

- Feeding and watering instructions—amounts and times
- Cage cleaning instructions
- Health issues or medications
- Veterinarian's name, address and phone number

- Rabbit expert contact—experienced rabbit owner or fellow club member
- Phone number and location where you can be reached
- Other household duties that need to be done while you're gone

dent about leaving your pets in her care.

CARING FOR YOUR SENIOR RABBIT

A good diet, attention to hygiene, and adequate exercise will help ensure a long, healthy life for your bunny. For many rabbits, this means a life span comparable to that of dogs, 10 to 12 years. Thanks to your pet's naturally high-strung temperament, you may not even notice that your rabbit is getting older.

Older rabbits can often appear just as sprightly as younger ones, but be assured that your pet is indeed aging, and there may be some health issues that inevitably accompany the later years. It pays to be especially observant of your bunny as he gets older. When your aged rabbit appears to be suffering instead of enjoying life, it may be time to gently and humanely say good-bye.

SAYING GOOD-BYE

Saying good-bye to a special animal friend is never an easy task. But then, watching a cherished pet suffer isn't any easier. When your rabbit's life has become filled with more pain than fun, when he is constantly sick and depressed, or when his physical state has left him with little quality of life, you can minimize your pet's suffering with euthanasia.

EUTHANASIA: Euthanasia is a word that means "good death." It is facilitated by an injection of drugs, administered by your veterinarian. Rather than having your pet endure prolonged suffering before death, euthanasia allows him to fall gently and painlessly to sleep. The drugs' effects are immediate, and within a few minutes of falling asleep, your rabbit's heart will stop beating.

It is difficult to make the decision to euthanize a beloved animal, but you should never feel guilty about sparing your innocent pet a lot of needless suffering. Your rabbit counts on you to do what is right for him, even when it is not easy to do so.

COPING WITH LOSS: The loss of your pet may be a very personal thing, or it may affect your entire family. It is important to recognize and acknowledge that each person handles grief in his or her own way. Some coping strategies you might want to consider include constructing a memorial for your pet, turning your loss into something positive, or redirecting your focus.

A memorial can be anything that helps preserve the fond memories you have of your bunny.

Constructing a photo collage, placing a garden stone, or even planting a tree in your pet's honor are all great ways to memorialize a special animal friend.

You can turn your loss into something positive by donating to a worthy animal cause in your pet's memory. You can volunteer your time and experience to help care for homeless bunnies. If you don't plan to get a new bunny any time soon, you can donate your pet's unused food and supplies to a local bunny rescue group.

At some point, you may realize that focusing too much on your loss does not help ease the pain. Instead, try to focus your time and attention on the other people and animals in your life, because your time with each of them is precious, too. Make plans for the future—a fun activity, a project to work on, a vacation or

It's never easy to lose a pet. However, you can help yourself heal by putting together a memoral garden or by placing a special marker where your pet is buried.

It may help to look at old photographs after your rabbit's passing.

trip—to give yourself something to look forward to.

Perhaps your future includes another chance to build a decade of memories with a new bunny. Take your time and make sure you're ready to open your heart and your home to another long-eared fellow before you take the plunge. Then, relish the excitement of starting anew.

❧❧❧

The greatest treasures of rabbit ownership are being able to see the world through a rabbit's eyes, to learn a new language called rabbit-speak, and to experience the rewards of bunny bonding. Much understanding can be gained from the friendship of such a small creature, and in the end, those whose lives have been rabbit-enriched are much better people because of it.

Organizations to Contact

American Animal Hospital Association (AAHA)
P.O. Box 150899
Denver, CO 80215-0899
Phone: 303-986-2800
Web site: www.aahanet.org

American Holistic Veterinary Medical Association (AHVMA)
2218 Old Emmorton Road
Bel Air, MD 21015
Phone: 410-569-0795
Web site: www.ahvma.org

American Rabbit Breeders Association (ARBA)
8 Westport Court
Bloomington, IL 61702
Phone: 309-664-7500
Web site: www.arba.net
E-mail: info@arba.net

American Society for the Prevention of Cruelty to Animals (ASPCA)
424 East 92nd Street
New York, NY 10128-6804
Phone: 212-876-7700
Web site: www.aspca.org

American Veterinary Medical Association
1931 North Meacham Road, Suite 100
Schaumburg, IL 60173-4360
Phone: 847-925-8070
Fax: 847-925-1329
Web site: www.avma.org
E-mail: avmainfo@avma.org

Association of Exotic Mammal Veterinarians (AEMV)
P.O. Box 396
Weare, NH 03281-0396
Fax: 478-757-1315
Web site: www.aemv.org
E-mail: info@aemv.org

Canadian Federation of Human Societies
102-30 Concourse Gate
Ottawa, Ontario, Canada
K2E 7V7
Phone: 613-224-8072
Toll free: 888-678-CFHS
E-mail: info@cfhs.ca
Web site: www.cfhs.ca

Delta Society
875 124th Ave. NE, Suite 101
Bellevue, WA 98005
Phone: 425-226-7357
Web site: www.deltasociety.org

**House Rabbit Society
International Headquarters &
Rabbit Center**
148 Broadway
Richmond, CA 94804
Phone: 510-970-7575
Web site: www.rabbit.org

**Humane Society of the
United States**
2100 L St., NW
Washington, DC 20037
Phone: 202-452-1100
Web site: www.hsus.org

**National Association of
Professional Pet Sitters (NAPPS)**
17000 Commerce Parkway, Suite C
Mt. Laurel, NJ 08054
Phone: 856-439-0324
Web site: www.petsitters.org

**National 4-H Headquarters
U.S. Dept. of Agriculture**
1400 Independence Ave., SW,
Stop 2225
Washington, D.C. 20250-2225
Phone: 202-720-2908
Web site: www.national4-h
          headquarters.gov

Pet Loss Support Hotline
College of Veterinary Medicine
Cornell University
Ithaca, NY 14853-6401
Phone: 607-253-3932
Web site: www.vet.cornell.edu/
          public/petloss

Pet Sitters International (PSI)
201 East King Street
King, NC 27021-9161
Phone: 336-983-9222
Web site: www.petsit.com

Further Reading

Fox, Sue. *Animal Planet Pet Care Library: Rabbits.* Neptune City, N.J.: T.F.H. Publications, 2006.

Harriman, Marinell. *The House Rabbit Handbook: How to Live with an Urban Rabbit.* 4th ed. Alameda, Calif.: Drollery Press, 2005.

Moore, Lucile, and Kathy Smith. *When Your Rabbit Needs Special Care: Traditional and Alternative Healing Methods.* Santa Monica, Calif.: Santa Monica Press, 2008.

Orr, Joan and Teresa Lewin. *Getting Started: Clicking with Your Rabbit.* Waltham, Mass.: Sunshine Books, 2006.

Pavia, Audrey. *Rabbits for Dummies.* New York: Wiley Publishing, 2003.

Standard of Perfection. American Rabbit Breeders Association, Inc.; Bloomington, IL, 2006.

Internet Resources

www.allearsac.org/poison.html

A comprehensive list of plants that are poisonous to rabbits, provided by the Sacramento House Rabbit Society.

www.arba.net

The American Rabbit Breeders Association is an organization dedicated to the care and development of rabbits in the United States and Canada.

www.aemv.org/vetlist.cfm

The Association of Exotic Mammal Veterinarians directory of veterinarians is searchable by state and includes a listing of what species a given veterinarian treats.

www.avma.org/careforanimals/animatedjourneys/ goodbyefriend/goodbye.asp

The American Veterinary Medical Association's grief resource site contains helpful information and guidance about the loss of a pet, including a listing of pet loss support hotlines.

http://extension.oregonstate.edu/catalog/pdf/pnw/pnw310-e.pdf

An excellent, printable publication on the diseases and parasites that affect domestic rabbits, produced by Oregon State University.

www.petfinder.com

This Web site provides information about adoptable rabbits from shelters across the country.

www.petinsurance.com/index.aspx

Veterinary Pet Insurance (VPI) is the number-one recommended veterinary pet insurance, with policies available for almost any kind of pet, including small mammals.

www.petsit.com

The Pet Sitters International Web site contains a listing of certified pet sitters as well as helpful information on choosing a pet sitter. The searchable database is easy to use, and has an option to search for sitters who will take care of exotic pets.

www.rabbit.org/kids/index.html

A great source of information and activities for children, offered by the House Rabbit Society.

www.woodworkersworkshop.com/resources/index.php?cat=453

A collection of Do-it-Yourself building plans for rabbit hutches and cages gleaned from various sites around the Internet.

Index

Numbers in **bold italics** refer to captions.

Contributors

JANICE BINIOK has written numerous articles and several books on companion animals. She has an English degree from the University of Wisconsin–Milwaukee and is a member of the Dog Writers Association of America, Inc. Janice lives on a small farm in Waukesha, Wisconsin, with her husband, two sons, and several four-legged members of the family.

Senior Consulting Editor **GARY KORSGAARD, DVM,** has had a long and distinguished career in veterinary medicine. After graduating from The Ohio State University's College of Veterinary Medicine in 1963, he spent two years as a captain in the Veterinary Corps of the U.S. Army. During that time he attended the Walter Reed Army Institute of Research and became Chief of the Veterinary Division for the Sixth Army Medical Laboratory at the Presidio, San Francisco.

In 1968 Dr. Korsgaard founded the Monte Vista Veterinary Hospital in Concord, California, where he practiced for 32 years as a small animal veterinarian. He is a past president of the Contra Costa Veterinary Association, and was one of the founding members of the Contra Costa Veterinary Emergency Clinic, serving as president and board member of that hospital for nearly 30 years.

Dr. Korsgaard retired in 2000, and currently enjoys golf, hiking, international travel, and spending time with his wife Susan and their three children and four grandchildren.